CONTENTS

SLOWING MILITARY CHANGE

Zhivan J. Alach

October 2008

This manuscript was funded by the U.S. Army War College External Research Associates Program. Information on this program is available on our website, *www.StrategicStudiesInstitute. army.mil*, at the Publishing button.

*****

Comments pertaining to this report are invited and should be forwarded to: Director, Strategic Studies Institute, U.S. Army War College, 122 Forbes Ave, Carlisle, PA 17013-5244.

*****

All Strategic Studies Institute (SSI) publications are available on the SSI homepage for electronic dissemination. Hard copies of this report also may be ordered from our homepage. SSI's homepage address is: *www.StrategicStudiesInstitute.army.mil*.

*****

The Strategic Studies Institute publishes a monthly e-mail newsletter to update the national security community on the research of our analysts, recent and forthcoming publications, and upcoming conferences sponsored by the Institute. Each newsletter also provides a strategic commentary by one of our research analysts. If you are interested in receiving this newsletter, please subscribe on our homepage at *www.StrategicStudiesInstitute.army. mil/newsletter/*.

ISBN 1-58487-367-1

FOREWORD

All actions begin from an evaluation of the environment. If our perceptions of the environment are flawed, then our actions flow from error. This is especially important in the military field, given the lives that are in danger if our actions are mistaken, as well as the heavy financial cost associated with equipment, personnel, and training. Unfortunately, it appears that many evaluations of the contemporary military environment are based on a flawed perception of that environment.

This monograph revises, reexamines, and reevaluates the contemporary military environment. It finds that the environment is a period of relative military stasis, of slow technological development, and of little novelty in broader issues. If anything, it is a return to an older period, of the time before the Cold War, before the fear of nuclear war dominated all other thinking in the field. This monograph is a first step in a broader and more incisive revision of contemporary strategic thought.

Douglas C. Lovelace, Jr.

DOUGLAS C. LOVELACE, JR.
Director
Strategic Studies Institute

BIOGRAPHICAL SKETCH OF THE AUTHOR

ZHIVAN J. ALACH is a capability analyst within the General Staff, New Zealand Army. He is currently working on a historical monograph analyzing New Zealand's participation in peace support operations over the past 50 years. He has published articles in several journals, focusing on evolution and change within militaries. Dr. Alach holds a Ph.D. in Defence Policy from the University of Auckland, focusing on post-Cold War defense policies in Australia and New Zealand, and how they have responded to an evolving strategic environment. He also holds a Postgraduate Diploma in Defence and Strategic Studies from Massey University and the New Zealand Military Studies Institute.

SUMMARY

This monograph looks at the development of military technology in recent years. It examines three major platforms: fighter aircraft, tanks, and cruisers, examining the gaps between generations as well as the capability gains of each succeeding type. While it shows that development has slowed, at the same time capability increases have also slowed: it takes longer to get new equipment, and that new equipment is less of an improvement over its predecessor than its predecessor was over its predecessor. It is thus a period of declining gains. Only in electronics and computer technology was that thesis shown to be somewhat untrue, but even there military technology has lagged significantly behind commercial advances, and thus to call it innovative and rapidly developing is to draw a long bow. This *relative military stasis*, in technology, at least, has a range of causes: the end of the Cold War, bureaucratic changes, political cultures, scientific limits, cost inflation, a focus on new characteristics that cannot be so easily measured. The monograph also looks at the strategic environment to see whether that has evolved rapidly while technology has proven more dormant. While many of the issues that characterize the post-Cold War period were also present during the Cold War; they may be newly important, but they are not necessarily new. Indeed, the contemporary period may be seen as a return to military normalcy after the lengthy anomaly of the Cold War. It is a shift away from state-on-state conflict, away from large scale war, away from a view that sees armies as forces designed solely for decisive, Clausewitzian battles. Yes, there has been change since the end of the Cold War, but it should not be exaggerated; rather than innovation, it might be taken as reaction, and the Cold War should be examined from a new perspective as a period of radical innovation in strategic terms, which would further be reinforced by the rapid technological development that characterized it.

This monograph, as the centerpiece of its method, examines the development of a range of military systems; one of the most indicative of these is the F/A-22. The F/A-22 is expected to remain in service until 2050; this will be 66 years since the detailed requirements for the Advanced Tactical Fighter were set. This is a long time in military history; 66 years ago, a fighter known as the P-51 was entering service. That is an argument from extremes, but it is still valid nonetheless. Today's military environment moves slowly; let us be willing to accept that, rather than assume that because it is our environment, it must somehow be more innovative than those that have gone before. Let us use the time that this relative military stasis affords us to examine the strategic environment both more closely and from a greater distance.

SLOWING MILITARY CHANGE

INTRODUCTION

It seems to be a commonplace today among strategic and military analysts that we are in a time of rapid, world-altering change.[1] The military environment is evolving swiftly, they say; some even believe we are witnessing a full-scale revolution in military affairs (RMA). Conflicts in Iraq and Afghanistan are seen as "fourth generation" warfare, by definition distinct from anything that has gone before. Modern technologies, from the F/A-22 *Raptor*, through robotic bomb disposal systems, to personal weapons, are seen as pushing the boundaries of capability far beyond those that existed but a few years ago. Even as we speak, it seems, defense forces are making quantum gains in military effectiveness through the acquisition of new weapons and the communications and control systems required to integrate them. Concomitant with this rapid progress is rapid obsolescence; each system is swiftly superceded by its successor, and if a force does not jump onto the "elevator of progress," it runs the risk of being left behind in a sort of military backwater, a Swiss Guard writ large. This military acceleration is seen as part of similar development around the world, whether it be how social interactions are being shaped by the internet, or how global trade patterns have adapted and shifted as a response to new policies and technologies. Some have gone so far as to call the contemporary strategic environment "global chaos."[2] A cursory look at some of the futurist projections of defense analysts shows that many expect such world-altering trends to strengthen in the future, creating an unstable and dangerous world full of asymmetric threats, international crime, and extremism-fueled terrorism.[3] In such an environment, it is not merely equipment that can become obsolescent, but also mindsets, exemplified by planning to fight the last war, rather than the next.

The question that poses itself to the author is whether or not the above analyses are truly the case. Have we instead committed a basic human fallacy in assuming that there is something unique about our generation that was somehow lacking in the myriad previous generations that stretch back into pre-history? This perspective is a sort of distorted presentism, and it is understandable: we cannot see the past, but we can see the present, and thus we assume greater distinctiveness about that which we can perceive. A good example of this is public perception of the standards of contemporary youth behaviour. The first months of 2008 have been full of political posturing and public comment about the declining standards of New Zealand's youth.[4] They are seen as more violent, more disrespectful, less educated, less well-spoken, and generally a devolution from the youth of the past. Unfortunately, the value of such assertions is reduced by the fact that every generation criticises the declining moral standards of its youth.[5] The parents of the 1960s were shocked by the sexual promiscuity of their free-love embracing teenagers. The parents of the 1920s were concerned about the dance crazes sweeping much of the western world. Medieval moralists thought society was on the path to destruction, and if we go back just a little further, we find two marvellous quotes that might easily have come from the mouth of Leader of the Opposition John Key or Prime Minister Helen Clark:

The children now love luxury; they have bad manners, contempt for authority; they show disrespect for elders and love chatter in place of exercise. Children are now tyrants, not the servants of their households. They no longer rise when elders enter the room. They contradict their parents, chatter before company, gobble up dainties at the table, cross their legs, and tyrannize their teachers.[6]

I see no hope for the future of our people if they are dependent on the frivolous youth of today, for certainly all youth are reckless beyond words. When I was a boy, we were taught to be discrete and respectful of elders, but the present youth are exceedingly wise and impatient of restraint.[7]

The former is attributed to the Greek philosopher, Socrates, and is approximately 2,400 years old; the latter to Hesiod. They show that either youth standards have indeed declined every generation, which surely would have led to the destruction of human civilization by marauding teenagers at some stage in the past, or that our comments about those standards are flawed and subjective. More objective measurements, such as statistics on youth crime, teenage pregnancy, drug use, literacy, and educational achievement, provide much better evidence with which to either criticise or compliment the moral standards of any particular youth generation. The use of such semi-objective criteria for measurement avoids the distorted presentism mentioned before, the tendency to believe strongly in the uniqueness and distinctiveness of one's own generation without truly examining such assertions in the light of the historical context.

This monograph is a reevaluation of the thesis that we are in a time of rapid military change. It might be called revisionist strategic analysis. Its broad conclusion can be stated simply: we are in a period of *relative military stasis* when compared to developments of approximately the past 150 years. This monograph comes to that conclusion through an analysis of technological change across a range of systems and countries, as well as an examination of the evolving character of the strategic environment. The monograph is a broad-brush treatment, and for good reasons: to identify the nature of change (or lack thereof) within an entire system requires a very broad perspective, lest a point that is true in the general be criticized because it does not explain a specific issue. A second reason is length. All macro analyses, by definition, are simplifications, but they are no less true for being so. This monograph touches on several issues of theory and detail that are deserving of much closer attention and lengthier works, but that is for a later date. It avoids making policy recommendations for the very simple reason that to do so would add yet another analytical stage to the piece and would thus lengthen it further. It is enough merely to suggest that contemporary interpretations of the military-strategic environment require substantial rethinking if they are to withstand critical cross-examination, and to make some minor recommendations for further work in the area.

A REPRESENTATIVE PROGRAM — THE F-22

Let us start by examining what seems at first glance a strong counter to my argument that military change has stagnated: the F/A-22 *Raptor*, the world's most advanced fighter.[8] It is the world's first stealthy, super-cruise capable fighter, and is claimed to be an order of magnitude more capable than contemporary fighters, if exercise kill models are to be believed.[9] Such capability has been very long in coming. The F/A-22 has its roots in the Advanced Tactical Fighter (ATF) competition, whose initial requirements were set in 1981, 27 years ago. More detailed requirements were set in 1984, and a Request For Proposals (RFP) was issued in 1986. The YF-22 prototype had its first flight in 1990, 6 years after the requirements were set down, and won the competition to be America's next-generation fighter the following year (1991), beating the rival Northrop YF-23. In August of that year, a contract to produce 11 F/A-22s was signed. The first part of the first aircraft was completed in December 1993; by 1995, mid-body, wings, and forebody manufacturing began. In December 1996, the aircraft was under full electrical power. Taxi tests were undertaken in August and September 1997, and the first flight of the first production F/A-22 took place on September 7, 1997. The recommendation to proceed with Low Rate Initial Production (LRIP) was given in August 2001, and the first F/A-22 squadron was stood up in October 2002. Initial Operating Capability (IOC) was reached on December 15, 2005.

The above may seem like an overly detailed list of dates and details, but it is important to understand the sheer length of time that has been involved in the development of the F/A-22. From the initial formulation of requirements to IOC took 24 years. From RFP to IOC took 19 years. The first flight of the prototype F/A-22 and the first flight of the production F/A-22 were separated by 7 years. It took another 8 years after the first flight of the production F/A-22 for IOC to be achieved. When one considers the number of people that have worked on the F/A-22, it is apparent that its phenomenal capability has come at the price of many thousands, perhaps a million, man-years.

Much has changed in the world since the initial formulation of requirements for the F/A-22. In 1981, the President of the United States was Ronald Reagan, and the Prime Minister of New Zealand was Robert Muldoon. The military-strategic environment was dominated by fears of nuclear war, and Afghanistan was sending a chill through superpower relations after a brief period of détente. Since then, the United States has gone through three more Presidents (and will soon have a fourth), and New Zealand has seen seven more Prime Ministers on the Treasury benches. China, rather than the Soviet Union, has become the greatest threat to American power. It is rather unlikely that Russian tanks will stream through the Fulda Gap on a few hours notice, protected by an umbrella of Su-27s that requires the attentions of the F/A-22. The above points should not be seen as asserting that the F/A-22 has no relevance to the contemporary environment; that is far from the truth, and later examination of the strategic environment will indicate that. The sheer capability envelope of the F/A-22 grants it the flexibility to operate in almost any sort of military environment. The point is that technological development has lagged substantially behind changes in the global situation.

Let us now go back into time to examine what was the F/A-22 of its day, the North American P-51 *Mustang*. The P-51 is perhaps the second most recognisable of all World War II fighters, behind only the *Spitfire*.[10] Its range revolutionized the European air war, allowing heavy bombers to fly escorted to their targets. Interestingly, this most American of aircraft had its roots in a British visit to North American Aviation (NAA) in April 1940.

The British were interested in NAA building P-40 *Warhawks* for the Royal Air Force (RAF). NAA, feeling that they could do better, instead offered to build an entirely new fighter. Within 117 days of that decision being taken, an engine-less prototype was ready. Six weeks later, and now with an Allison engine, the P-51 took its first flight. By April 1942, some initial Allison-engined P-51s were flying reconnaissance missions, and by September of that year, a new *Merlin*-engined prototype took to the air. By the end of the war in 1945, P-51 models from A to H had fought. Nearly each variant introduced some new technology, such as the bubble canopy, and the base P-51 itself had itself been a major leap forward in aerodynamics due to its laminar flow wing design.

This was indeed rapid technological development. It took only 2 years from initial requirements to operational capability. Within 2 years of the first prototype flying, a variant with an entirely new powerplant was in the air. At first glance, then, the case of the P-51 seems to show very clearly that military development has slowed significantly in roughly half a century. Had the P-51 followed the same path as the F/A-22, it would have become operational in 1964.

Some readers might suggest that comparison of the F/A-22 and P-51 is not valid, because one was a rushed, wartime program, when the degree of threat demanded rapid technological development to meet new demands, and when funds were more freely available.[11] Others might suggest that the differing level of complexity between the P-51 and F/A-22 renders the comparison flawed. Such assertions are not counters; they are explanations. The fact that a reason for a delay exists does not alter the reality of the delay itself. However, a stronger counter might be that this comparison is an anomaly, and that other systems do not show such disparity in development times. It is useful to strengthen and deepen the argument, and ensure it is not an argument from extremes, by examining a broad range of 20th century military technological projects to see whether or not the comparison of the P-51 and F/A-22 holds up against the evidence. In order to do so, this monograph examines three main systems across several countries: American fighters, Soviet tanks, and surface ships, especially cruisers.[12] The rationale for the focus on the United States and the Soviet Union is simple: as the world's primary superpowers during the period of study, it was they who were at the forefront of military technological advancement.[13]

DEVELOPMENT OF AMERICAN FIGHTERS

Analysis of American fighter aircraft will be divided into two sections. In the first, development times will be analyzed; in the second, performance gains from succeeding generations will be examined. This will thus illustrate whether development times have lengthened as well as whether or not performance gains have mirrored development timeframes.[14]

Development Times.

The first aircraft we shall examine is the Boeing P-26 *Peashooter*, which in its day was regarded as a sophisticated technological advance over existing fighters.[15] The initial concept for the P-26 was formulated in 1931; a prototype flew in 1932, and it entered service in 1933.

A few years later, in 1937 specifically, the first concepts for what was to become the P-40 *Warhawk* were put down.[16] Three years later it had its first flight. We shall avoid analysis of World War II developments, to avoid accusations that wartime development is anomalous, and take up the tale again in the post-war period with the first generation of jet fighters. In 1946, the prototype for the F-84 was developed, and it entered operational service the next year.[17] Its stablemate, the F-86, was first conceptualised in 1944.[18] A prototype flew in 1947, a production version the next year, and it achieved IOC in 1949, introducing the swept wing into U.S. Air Force (USAF) service.

However, experience in Korea showed the limitations of even such an advanced aircraft, and in 1952 a new design, which became the F-104, was developed to ensure American air superiority.[19] A prototype flew in 1954, and by 1956 the F-104 was in USAF service. As will be seen below, despite this swift development timeframe, the F-104 provided substantial increases in performance over its predecessors. Yet it, too, was swiftly superceded: its successor, the F-4 *Phantom* was birthed, on paper at least, in 1953; it flew by 1958, and entered service in 1961.[20] Within 4 years, however, the USAF felt it needed an even better fighter. A design contest was held from 1965 to 1967 to develop that next generation aircraft: it became the F-15 *Eagle*.[21] The *Eagle* first flew in 1972, and entered service in 1975. But the F-15 was expensive, and in order to provide a low-cost alternative, the USAF launched the Lightweight Fighter Program (LFP) in 1972. The winner of this was the YF-16, which became the F-16; the defeated competitor was the YF-17. A prototype F-16 was ready in 1975, and a production version took its first flight a year later.[22] It entered service in 1979. The YF-17, however, did not die. It was modified into what became the F/A-18. The first F/A-18 prototype was ready by 1978, and it achieved IOC in 1982.[23] In the 26 years since, however, only one other American fighter has entered service: the F/A-22.

The above summary is dense and number-heavy, but it is necessary. It shows quite clearly that development times have been elongating for decades. The P-26 took a couple of years to go from paper to service; the P-40, 3 years. The F-86 took only 5 years despite the fact that it incorporated a revolutionary new powerplant and much data gained from the freshly conquered Germans. The F-104 went from concept to service in 4 years, the F-4 in 8 years, and the F-15 took a decade. The F-16 took 7 years, and the F/A-18, despite losing a major competition, took only 3 more years than the F-16. At most, American fighter programs before the F/A-22 took half the time that the F/A-22 has taken.

Performance Gains.

Development times do not tell the full story, as they do not indicate the gain in performance achieved by each succeeding generation. A system might take twice as long to develop but be twice as capable, and as such could not truly be regarded as a slowing of capability advance. But, at least when measured by the most obvious performance criteria for fighter aircraft, there has been a concomitant decrease in performance enhancement even as development times have lengthened: in simple terms, it takes longer to get less.

Aircraft	IOC	Speed (kmh) (meters)	Ceiling	Range (km)	Load (kg)
P-26[24]	1933	377	8,354	1022	91
P-40[25]	1940	609	11,585	1352	682
F-84[26]	1947	1,119	14,024	1385	2,727
F-104[28]	1948	1,138	13,902	1344	2,364
F-4[29]	1961	2,415	18,293	2093	5,682
F-15[30]	1975	3,019	19,817	3700	4,091-10,909
F-16[31]	1979	2,415	15,244	3885	10,000-15,000
F/A-18[32]	1982	2,190	15,244	3700	6,227

Table 1. Fighter Speeds, Ceilings, Ranges, and Warloads.

Table 1 shows speed, ceiling, range, and warload, which are crucial determinants of fighter capability, measured against year of service. They show that during the early and middle period of the timeframe concerned, performance increases from generation to generation were very substantial. The F-84 and F-86 introduced jet propulsion and other advanced features and increased the speed of American fighters by a factor of 1.4 to 1.87 or so. Yet, despite this major improvement in performance, they were developed in a handful of years at most. With the F-104, performance rocketed even more. It increased speed by a factor of 1.87 over the first generation jets. From 1945 to 1956, the top speed of American fighter aircraft almost tripled, from the 720kmh achievable by a P-51H, to the 2125kmh of the F-104. In later years, there has been a tailing off in performance in these criteria, and it is noticeable that the F-16 and F/A-18 are actually less capable than the F-15.

The greatest increases in performance came with swiftly developed systems. The aircraft that took the longest to develop, such as the F-15 and F/A-18, improved speed, range, ceiling, and warload only slightly over the preceding generation. Indeed, there seems to be an inverse relationship between development time and performance gain, which is approximated in Figure 1:

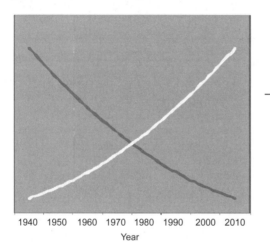

Figure 1. Development Time vs. Performance Gain.

Of course, criteria of speed, range, and ceiling do not tell the whole story. It is possible that development has occurred in areas that are not measured above. A method to identify such development(s) is to move away from the platforms and examine when specific technologies entered operational service. This sort of analysis may illustrate some issues that the above, broad-brush, survey does not.

The first true fire-and-forget air-to-air missile was the *Sidewinder*, which entered service in the late 1950s.[33] The first fighter with true look-down-shoot-down capability was the F-15, which as noted earlier entered service in 1975.[34] The first operational fly-by-wire (FBW) aircraft was the F-16 *Falcon* of 1979.[35] The first stealth aircraft was the F-117 *Nighthawk*, which achieved IOC by 1983.[36] Since then, the only major aeronautical innovation has been supercruise in the F/A-22. While there have been major developments in electronics, including computers and communications equipment, they are not specific to aircraft, and they are discussed in a later section. In those areas specific to aircraft, it is clear that performance has slowed. To see whether this is an anomaly amongst broader military trends, it is illustrative to look at another major weapons system: the tank.[37] Specifically, Soviet tank development will be examined using the same framework as used for American fighter aircraft.

DEVELOPMENT OF SOVIET TANKS

Wartime development of Soviet tanks, from the T-34 and KV-1 through to the T-44 and IS-3, will be passed over.[38] The story will be taken up in 1946, when the prototype of the T-54 was first produced.[39] Three years later, it entered operational service. A successor, the T-55, was built on many of the same components, and reached the prototype stage in 1957. It was made operational in 1958. A much more advanced tank, the T-62, also reached the prototype stage in 1957, but it did not enter service until 1961-62.[40] In 1962, the T-64 tank reached the prototype stage, entering operational service in 1966.[41] Due to its complexity and cost, a lower-price alternative, the T-72, was developed from 1967,[42] entering service in 1971.[43] The T-80, the T-72's successor, was actually developed from the T-64.[44] Its prototype was built in 1976, and 2 years later, production tanks were entering service units. Since then, as with American fighters, there has been a substantial pause, and the latest in-service Russian/ Soviet tank, the T-90, was first conceptualized in 1988, entering service in 1993.[45] Since then, while there have been prototypes, variants, and concept vehicles, there has been no new in-service tank. Table 2 shows the approximate development timeline of Russian tanks.

Tank	Prototype	Service	Time to Service
T-54[46]	1946	1949	3 years
T-55[47]	1957	1958	1 year
T-62[48]	1957	1961-1962	4-5 years
T-64[49]	1962	1966	4 years
T-72[50]	1967	1971	4 years
T-80[51]	1976	1978	2 years
T-90[52]	1988	1993	5 years

Table 2. Russian Tank Development Timelines.

The above chronology is more complex than that for American fighters. The time taken from prototype to service has not lengthened, and indeed for the T-80, it shortened. Some care must be taken here, however, as dates may be a year or two out, and with the short time frames being discussed, a small error can have seemingly major consequences. What is more apparent, instead, is that the gap between generations of tanks reaching the prototype stage has steadily increased, bar the anomaly of the T-54 and T-55.[53] The gap between the T-62 and T-64 prototypes was 5 years; between the T-64 and T-72, 5 years; between the T-72 and T-80, 9 years; and between the T-80 and T-90, 12 years. The 20 years since have not seen a single new Russian tank.

Technologically, development has also slowed. The first generation T-54 and T-55 had 100mm rifled guns, which were superceded by much more powerful smoothbore technology in the T-62.[54] All Soviet tanks since that time have used smoothbore cannons in 115mm or 125mm calibers, and although ballistic performance has improved, the same basic concept has remained.[55] Range has not greatly improved: the T-54 was capable of 450km on internal fuel, the T-72 of 500km, and the T-90 supposedly capable of 600km. Armor protection evolved rapidly during the early part of the period, from sloped steel armor on the first three (T-54, T-55, and T-62) through to first generation composites on the T-64 and more advanced materials from the T-72 onwards, including reactive armor and active defense systems.

Even more than with the fighters examined above, it is important to look at specific tank technologies. Explosive reactive armor (ERA), for example, was first developed by the Israelis and was operational by 1982.[56] Within a few years, Russian tanks were carrying first-generation ERA as well, and heavy types were developed by the early 1990s. The first Russian gun-tube-launched anti-tank missile was mounted in the T-64B of 1976, though an American system called *Shillelagh* had come into service in the 1960s.[57] Active defense systems were first installed on the T-55 in 1983,[58] and more sophisticated systems were in service by the early 1990s.[59] Russian tank development is a clear indication of incrementalism. The basics of their turret shape, armament, and complex armor package have changed only in degree, rather than kind, since the T-64. There have been constant improvements, but no quantum leaps, bar concepts such as the *Black Eagle* experimental tank.[60] It might be said that for the past 40 years or so, all Russian tanks have been merely "children and grandchildren"[61] of the T-64, which is hardly a sign of technological innovation.

Readers familiar with Russian tank development may counter that such incrementalism is a traditional Russian practice: rather than producing an entirely new design, Russian designers often modify an existing system. This leads to an alphabet soup of variants, exemplified by the following types of T-72, which is not even an exhaustive list: T-72A, T-72B, T-72BK, T-72BM, T-72M, T-72M1, T-72S, T-72BV, and T-72SUO.[62] Thus, Russian tank development might be perceived as anomalous, or even if it is not anomalous, it might be considered that such incrementalism may well have led to rapid technological gains.

There are several counters to this. Against the first charge, that Russian incremental tank development is anomalous, the example of American tank development can be offered. American tank design followed a similar, incremental path for much of the post-World War II period. The M-46, M-47, M-48 and M-60 were merely incremental developments of the M-26 *Pershing*.[63] Only with the M-1 *Abrams* was a truly new concept trialed, and the *Abrams* was developed in the 1970s. All American tank development since then has been, as with the Russians, incremental improvements of an existing platform.[64] Against the second charge, it is quite true that incrementalism can lead to rapid technological change, if small gains are spaced closely apart.[65] However, the spacing between incremental gains has widened, rather than shortened. The T-90, for example, is much less of a capability gain over its predecessor, the T-80, than the T-62 was over the T-55 or the T-64 was over the T-62. The same relationship between performance gain and development time as seen with American fighters is apparent here, if to a lesser extent.

DEVELOPMENT OF CRUISERS

Let us move on from the air and land environments and briefly examine the sea to see whether similar historical trends are apparent. This section will focus on the development of large surface combatants, especially U.S. cruisers, but with mention of other countries.[66]

Our cursory survey begins in 1933 with the British *Leander*-class.[67] Her armament comprised eight 6" guns, and she could do 32.5 knots; as such, she was a representative pre-war cruiser. In 1939, the British began the *Dido*-class, and her fitout showed a distinct awareness of changing requirements: her armament was 10 5.25" dual-purpose (anti-surface and anti-aircraft) guns.[68] From 1942 to 1945, the United States introduced the *Cleveland*-class into service: they carried 12 152mm guns, but some units were also equipped with radar and a Combat Information Center (CIC), improvements that enhanced their warfighting capability substantially.[69] The *Des Moines* of 1948 had 203mm guns, but for the most part was little different from her wartime predecessors.[70] With the *Galveston*-class of 1958, however, American cruisers reached the missile age with *Talos* surface-to-air missiles (SAMs), at approximately the same time that USAF fighters were receiving their own guided missiles.[71] Three years later, the *Long Beach*, the world's first nuclear powered cruiser, entered service.[72] Several classes of cruisers followed with incremental improvements to fire control and armament, but it was not until the *Ticonderoga* class of 1983 that there was a substantial leap in cruiser capability.[73] This was due to the *Aegis* system, which massively improved the ability of ships to deal with air and surface threats. All major American surface vessels since 1983, bar carriers, have been *Aegis* ships, albeit with upgraded and improved systems. Some have replaced rail-launchers for missiles with Vertical Launch Systems (VLS), and many have received electronics upgrades. More innovative concepts for surface ships have been promulgated, but none have yet entered service.[74]

While the above three-pronged examination can only summarize military technological development over the past 50 years or so, it is still a very useful tool. It has focused on the two countries most often at the forefront of military development, the United States and Russia. It has focused on major weapons systems, fighters, tanks, and cruisers, where technological development can be clearly perceived if it occurs. What this analysis has shown, however, is that there has been a steady slowdown in the physical improvement of major weapons systems around the world, even as development times have lengthened. This is especially apparent in the period since 1990, as will be examined more closely later in this piece. The most advanced U.S. fighter, the F/A-22, was conceptualized 24 years ago. The latest Russian tank, the T-90, reached prototype stage 20 years ago. The basic design for contemporary American major surface units dates from 1983. A global survey of other systems would further reinforce these findings.[75] The Eurofighter was developed to Cold War requirements. The German *Leopard* 2's basic design is 30 years old. Tanks are not much more powerful, nor much more heavily armored, than they were 2 decades ago. Fighters are no faster, and scarcely more maneuverable, than they were 15 years ago. Ships do not carry weapons greatly more destructive than those they carried 25 years ago. In many cases, major platforms have stayed in service much longer than would have been the case earlier in the century, and many of them are intended to stay in service for several decades more. Development timelines stretch out endlessly due to requirements changes, cost overruns, or just poor planning.[76]

RELATIVE MILITARY STASIS — HISTORICAL COMPARISONS

One should pause now and state clearly that the message is not that the contemporary period is one of absolute military stagnation; rather, it is that compared to recent history, it is a time of *relative military stasis*. There are entire centuries of human existence when military progress in some fields was slower than it is today: for example, from 1700 to 1850, the technological character of land warfare scarcely changed.[77] However, there have also been periods — some centuries ago, others more recent — where military progress was much swifter than today.[78] It is those periods that put the lie to contemporary assertions about the chaotic, innovative nature of the current environment. Several counterexamples should serve to illustrate the point.

A good example is the latter part of the 19th century, a period when technological development — especially in metallurgy and machinery — led to a deliberate tendency to seek technological solutions to military-tactical problems.[79] Ironclad warships were obsolete almost the moment they hit the water, especially once HMS *Dreadnought* was launched;[80] indeed, the Royal Navy of the time was "relentless and extravagant" in demanding technological innovation.[81] Speed rocketed, range lengthened, armor thickened, and firepower grew immensely more devastating.[82] The earliest wireless sets began to be fitted at this time as well, revolutionizing command and control.[83] The Royal Navy was not the only navy to catch a "Victorian naval bug." The Japanese grew from 28 ships of 57,000 combined tons in 1894 to 76 ships of 250,000 combined tons in 1903, as well as 76 torpedo boats.[84]

The French Revolution was a period of even more rapid military change, although more in the case of politico-strategy than technology or tactics. In 20 years, it turned a European society with very few soldiers into one that was "militarised from top to bottom," and in which service as a soldier became a common experience across an entire continent.[85] More confined was German military development in the 1930s. Germany went from seven infantry divisions and no combat aircraft in 1933 to 36 infantry divisions and three panzer divisions by 1937, with 3,350 combat aircraft by the year after.[86] Wartime development, expansion, and evolution can be even more rapid.

History thus shows us many periods of truly rapid military progress, and it pays to keep those in mind when we seek to assess the contemporary period.[87] Steam and steel revolutionized the latter part of the 19th century;[88] in the 1930s, the integration of new communications equipment, existing technology, and innovative operational concepts revolutionized rates of advance in warfare; and the late 1940s and 1950s saw the emergence of quirky, futurist concepts that in turn helped massively improve the performance of various military systems, especially combat aircraft.[89]

In one area of military technology, there does, however, seem to have been rapid progress in recent years, which partially counters the arguments put forward earlier—the field of electronics, especially information technology and the integration of computers and communications devices. It is to this field that we now turn our eyes.

DEVELOPMENT OF INFORMATION TECHNOLOGY

The F-15 *Eagle* of 1975 had an IBM AP1 central processing unit (CPU) of approximately 1.3MHz and 64k memory.[90] The F/A-22 of 2005, on the other hand, has a Common Integrated Processor (CIP) with approximately 300Mb memory, roughly 5,000 times the memory of the F-15.[91] The F-35, which will enter service in the next decade, has an ICP system with a speed of 1-2GHz and easily expandable memory.[92] A mid-1980s Type 22 frigate had a *Seawolf* computer with 100kb memory and a close-in-weapons-system (CIWS) computer with 32kb memory; the shore command that controlled the frigate had a mainframe with but 10gb hard drive capacity, which is roughly 1-50th as large as the hard drive on which this article is being written.[93] Parallel to processor power improvements have been enhancements to data networks such as Information Processing (IP)-capable radios. Soldiers today often carry computers into battle, whether to collect and analyse information, communicate with headquarters, or control robotic flying vehicles. At first glance, this improvement in military computing technology seems quite spectacular; after all, how many other aspects of performance have seen 5,000-fold improvements in 30 years? A closer examination reveals, however, that military computing development has lagged substantially behind commercial development. While there is more rapid progress than in other aspects of military technology, it is progress pulled by commercial trends, rather than pushed by military research.

Moore's Law states that CPU power will double every 18 months, even as costs halve. This has largely been the case with commercial technology, and has even been exceeded. A standard desktop computer in 1991, when the F/A-22 won the ATF competition, might have a 12.5MHz processor, 1mb random access memory (RAM), and a 40mb hard drive.[94] A standard desktop computer in 2005, when the F/A-22 reached IOC, might have a 1.5GHz processor, 512Mb RAM, and 150gb of hard drive space.

The issue is whether military computing power has kept pace. It has not. The processor in an F/A-22 compares poorly to even a standard, commercial desktop system. The processors in an *Aegis*-class cruiser also compare quite poorly. "State of the art" in military computing terms is far from state of the art in commercial computing. The one exception is in major, fixed-site installations such as the code-breaking supercomputers used by the U.S. National Security Agency (NSA).

There are good reasons for this lag, including the need for ruggedization to ensure reliability under trying conditions, public sector purchasing methods, and the need to integrate computer technology into other military mechanical and electronic systems; none of these are the case in most commercial applications, and they will be examined later. But as stated earlier, the existence of reasons for a lag does not alter the fact that there is a lag, and that is the crucial issue. Traditionally, the military has led the commercial sector in the development of new technology due to the fact that the demands of war are usually such as to require the most advanced technology possible.[95] Military aircraft led the way with jet engines.[96] Piston engine technology, especially in relation to forced induction, was largely propelled by demands before and during World War II for greater high altitude performance.[97] The Global Positioning System (GPS) units that make it easy to drive around unfamiliar cities were developed primarily for military purposes.[98] Satellite television is an offshoot of space technology developed, again, for primarily military purposes. Advanced composite materials, which have made modern appliances and cars lighter and tougher, were often first developed for military aircraft and fighting vehicles. Today, however, the equation is reversed. Commercial innovation is passed onto military users.[99] It is retail customers for iPhones and Playstation 3s that set the tone, not general staffs and procurement executives.

It should also be clearly understood that what is sometimes seen as a revolution in military electronics is more correctly a revolution in computing technology only, especially processing power, storage capacity, and data transmission capacity. Electronic technology in broader terms has not necessarily developed at a particularly rapid rate in recent years. World War II, for example, saw the emergence of radar, active sonar, electronic countermeasures, electronic guidance systems, transponders, and guided missiles, all substantial advancements in the field of electronics. The post-war period saw less rapid growth, but still saw developments such as Advanced Research Projects Agency Network (ARPANET), the predecessor to the internet, electronically scanned arrays, and the first deployable data networks. We must then assign three qualifications to any portrayal of recent military electronic development as revolutionary: (1)

it is computer development, rather than across the broader field of electronics, (2) it is led by commercial imperatives, and (3) when examined in historical terms, it may not be as revolutionary as first perceived.

Even given these qualifications, however, the rapid rate of military computing development in comparison to other aspects of performance mentioned earlier does suggest that perhaps the criteria used to measure progress no longer tell the full story. Perhaps we should measure bandwidth capacity, processor speed, memory, and communications software rather than speed, range, and firepower. That is an issue that will be examined later, as it threatens the central finding of this work.

CAUSES OF RELATIVE MILITARY STASIS

The above sections comprise the first part of this piece, and they have described how the pace of military technological development has slowed, except in one major area, and even there, development has followed in the wake of commercial development. At times, the rationales for this *relative military stasis* have been touched on, but not to any great detail. The second part of this work, which follows, goes into those rationales to some depth. However, due to the size of this work, even that greater depth must be, by definition, relatively cursory.

Military change or stasis is the result of, at its most general and basic, three main factors:[100] the existence of an external threat, the culture of the state/government that controls a military, and the state of technology; in short: "threat," "culture," and "technology."[101] The first two especially are interlinked closely; any response to a threat will be shaped by culture, and external threats will in turn shape the culture of the state.[102] Evidence of the first can be seen in the differing ways different countries have responded to recent terrorism. Evidence of the second can be seen by comparing two countries such as Israel and New Zealand, whose military cultures have developed along very different paths due to different levels of threat. Technology can alter threat and also affect research and development. Within these three broad elements of threat, culture, and technology however, there are a range of subfactors determining change. In recent years, the character of those subfactors has been such as to slow the rate of military technological change.

Cause One: Darwinian Response.

The first reason for contemporary *relative military stasis*, which relates to the issue of threat, might be termed the "Darwinian thesis."[103] Military progress is analogous to organisms in an environmental system. Development occurs largely in response to external pressures and threats. During times when there is a major threat, especially wars,[104] technological evolution is rapid because systems are sought to ensure survival. The costs and potential failures resulting from such headlong development are proportionally less important because the external threat looms above all else.

The "Darwinian thesis" is not a simple action-reaction relationship between threat and response. As noted, the response to a threat is filtered by the culture of the state; it might be said that the existence of a threat usually determines that a response will be made, but the culture determines what that response will resemble.[105] Sometimes, military responses to external threats are so modified by the culture of the state that they seem to bear almost no resemblance to a rational countermeasure.[106] However, in the 20th and 21st centuries, those countries at the cutting edge of military technological development, especially the United States and Russia, have had militaries whose primary purpose has been the defense of the state against external enemies, and who have been controlled by governments who, at least in a bounded fashion, have attempted to respond to threats in rational manner.[107] Evidence of these boundedly rational responses is apparent in the history of the Cold War, some of which history has been touched on in the surveys earlier in this piece.

When the United States held a real fear of the Soviet Union, its superpower rival in the late 1940s and 1950s, it embarked on a frighteningly swift program of technological development, especially in the field of aircraft. Both nations threw vast resources into the development of intercontinental ballistic missiles (ICBM) during this period as well, with the spin-off being space technology; the Apollo program was the continuation of the Cold War by other means, fueled partly by propaganda requirements, partly by the types of equipment that had become available through missile programs. The Americans, fearful of the survivability of their existing bomber fleet of B-52s in the 1960s, attempted to develop a mach 3 bomber called the XB-70 *Valkyrie*.[108] The Soviets, fearful of the *Valkyrie*, developed a mach 3 fighter to intercept it, the MiG-25.[109] The Americans, and indeed all of NATO, fearful of a Soviet armored tide sweeping across the North German Plain, developed a range of light but powerful anti-tank guided missiles (ATGM) to restore some balance. To counter those ATGMs, Soviet tank designers developed ERA and both passive and active countermeasures suites. At sea, the Soviets were worried about the power of the U.S. carrier battle groups; they developed the concept of swarming attacks by dozens of bombers, each launching a pair of anti-ship missiles at long range, aiming to simply overwhelm defenses through numbers. To defeat such saturation attacks, American warships were equipped with the *Aegis* system. To defeat *Aegis*, the Soviets developed the *Sunburn* missile, capable of very-low-level supersonic flight.[110]

So it went on throughout the Cold War, a spiral of technological advancement fuelled largely by existential fear of one's superpower rival. Nor was the Cold War the only arms race in history: naval rivalry in the late 19th and early 20th centuries deserves the label, as does the headlong development of systems during World War II. Generally, when there is a clear and present external rival with both the motive and means to be of danger, military development is rapid.

The end of the Cold War removed such a clear and present threat from the strategic perspectives of most countries.[111] Superpower relations thawed, and a working relationship, tending occasionally to friendship, developed between the two power blocs after a half-century of antagonism and conflict. As relations improved, the possibility of global nuclear war receded. The two sides drew down the size of their nuclear arsenals and halted the practice of directly targeting each other's cities with strategic weapons. The process of nuclear weapons reduction continues today, with the positive end result that global nuclear war is now but a faint possibility, tending almost to the impossible.[112]

Conventional forces were also downsized from the early 1990s onwards, especially in Europe. The primary need for such large organizations, massive global war, had largely disappeared.[113] Economic constraints in the former Warsaw Pact nations, especially the Soviet Union and its primary successor state, Russia, also resulted in a withdrawal by those nations from political and military involvement around the globe. Confrontation fell away, not just in Europe, but also in Africa, the Middle East, Central America, and the high seas. Many conflicts around the globe had been proxy conflicts, wars fought by groups sponsored by the superpowers, and now that sponsorship, and with it the ability to make war, was withdrawn.[114]

Initially, this reduction in bipolar confrontation led to a widespread feeling of optimism with regard to global security. The first couple of years of the 1990s were a time of hope; some commentators believed that a new era of peace was about to develop around the world, stemming largely from the spread of representative democracy into nations formerly controlled by Communist ideologies.[115] The United Nations (UN), the preeminent institution of global peace and security, was liberated after almost half a century of being constrained by superpower rivalry.[116]

Such optimistic predictions have not come fully to pass, but it is a fact that the post-Cold War period has been less fraught with peril than was the Cold War. While there have been dangers, whether from terrorists or from ethnic conflict, such dangers have paled into insignificance when compared to the prospect of massive conventional or nuclear war between the two power blocs, even if it did not occur. As a result, the evolutionary impetus to develop new weapons systems has declined.

Especially important in this is the situation in Russia. From the 1930s onwards, the Soviet Union poured funds into military research, leading the world in several fields. When the Soviet Union collapsed, its successor states found themselves economically weak and facing serious fiscal constraints.[117] Russia, the largest and most powerful of the successor states, simply could not afford to keep spending such large amounts on military research. Military reform programs have thus been focused on economy and downsizing an over-large force; the United States is no longer seen as an ideological threat.[118] In recent years, especially under President Vladimir Putin, there has been an increase in defense funding, but even those amounts cannot compare to the levels available under the Soviet system. Many military industrial companies have been forced to coalesce into *de facto* marketing boards, or branch out into commercial development.[119] While concepts and prototypes abound, there is simply insufficient funding to turn them into service systems.[120] The focus has thus been on upgrading existing platforms incrementally, especially for export customers.[121]

The economic collapse of the Soviet Union had, in turn, major effects on the efforts of the United States, which was the other major military technological innovator. The primary threat to U.S. security had disappeared, and General Colin Powell, Chairman of the Joint Chiefs of Staff at the time, commented that it was difficult to know what to do when the "devil was dead."[122] Without a clear and present strategic danger, U.S. legislative fund providers wanted to take a "peace dividend" and reduce raw funding,[123] which severely impacted research and development budgets.[124] The F/A-22 program was delayed, reduced, and elongated by restricted funding.[125] Other advanced programs also suffered, as existing capabilities and operational deployments had to be funded from a suddenly smaller funding bucket. The number of B-2 *Spirit* stealth bombers to be purchased was reduced.[126] The RAH-66 *Comanche* next-generation attack helicopter program was cut, as was the *Crusader* artillery system.[127] Next-generation armored systems and aircraft have also been delayed under the pressure of smaller budgets.[128] More recently, expenditure on operations in Afghanistan and Iraq has also had an effect on U.S. military research and development, although not to the extent that might have been expected.[129] In other countries such as the United Kingdom, the effect of operational deployments in Iraq and Afghanistan has been much greater, with major next-generation programs in danger of delay or cancellation due to the pressure of funding operations from a limited budget.[130]

For much of the 20th century, the Soviet Union and United States were at the forefront of military evolution, pushing scientific boundaries with each generation. With the end of the Cold War, superpower rivalry disappeared; with that gone, the motivation for constant technological innovation also left. If Russia was not going to build a next generation fighter, then the United States did not need to think about a successor to the F/A-22. If the United States was not going to build a better tank than the *Abrams*, then Russia did not need to think about a successor to the T-90. This same interaction was repeated around the globe in many other countries, who saw the disappearance of a high-technology, high-motivation threat and with it the need for rapid technological development. What military demands did remain, such as peacekeeping and policing operations, did not demand the same technological sophistication as superpower war. Countries took peace dividends, stripping research, development, and production budgets, and with less money, it was simple: less work could be done. Further proof of this thesis can be seen in that some of the most rapid recent development in military technology has been in fields related to urgent operational requirements in Iraq and Afghanistan, showing the importance of a clear and present threat.[131]

The "Darwinian thesis," resting on the reduction in global tension and subsequent boundedly-rational responses of governments and militaries, accounts for much of contemporary *relative military stasis*, but not all of it. Signs of slowing military development were apparent before the end of the Cold War, especially from the mid 1970s onwards. This slowing spanned periods of increasing superpower rivalry, such as the period from 1979 to 1985, when it might have been expected, given the "Darwinian thesis" that research and development in response to external threats might increase. Indeed, U.S. President Ronald Reagan did institute a massive increase in defense funding against what he saw as the "Evil Empire" of the Soviet Union during the early 1980s, much of which was pumped into research and development. Yet this did not lead to substantial advances in operational military technology. The picture, therefore, has more parts, and cannot be explained monocausally. If threat were the only issue, then one could expect military development to have been slower in the 1970s during détente, than during the first part of the 1980s when the Cold War was rapidly cooling; this was not the case.[132]

Cause Two: Governmental Culture and Structure.

We now move onto what is best perceived as an element of culture: the role of governments and their internal structure. This factor is closely linked to the decline of tension in the post-Cold War period, but is still distinct in several crucial aspects.

In most of the world, the government controls the military, and in turn determines the direction of military research and development to a greater or lesser extent. While there are sophisticated interactions between the government, the military as a whole, the component services, and the industrial complex(es), by and large guidance flows from the top down, though as with every generalization, there are exceptions.[133] Governments provide funds, which determine which systems will be developed and procured: whoever controls the purse strings, controls the programs. As such, as governments change their internal structures, especially in the case of defense bureaucracies, there will be effects on the rate of development. A change in structure that streamlines procurement will speed up development; a change that makes procurement a lengthier process will slow down development.

One definite historical trend, which has survived the revisionism that has destroyed so many other perceived truths, is growth in the size and structural complexity of governments.[134] In the Middle Ages, central government might consist of a small court around a king or queen, with retainers scattered around the countryside as sheriffs or with similar duties. From the Renaissance onwards, central ministries developed, and by the 19th century, in advanced countries at least, the current structure of government had been achieved, albeit in a much smaller form. There were fewer bureaucrats and fewer departments, and less vertical depth. Despite the lack of communication technology in those times, decisions could be made quickly. The rapid development of warships in the United Kingdom in the latter part of the 19th century, noted earlier, proves this point.[135] For much of the first part of the 20th century, governments were smaller, decisions could be made more quickly, and there was a lesser demand for accountability from the media. In countries such as Fascist Germany and the Soviet Union, the primary goal of government was the achievement of military power, and as such the entire structure of the state was focused on military growth. In many cases, governments had state arsenals responsible for the development and production of weapons; as they had no other responsibilities, they were highly responsive and flexible in the circumstances of the time.[136]

Since World War II, however, governments around the world have become larger. This is a loaded political issue: leftists would say they provide essential services, rightists would call them bloated bureaucracies. The rightness or wrongness of "big government" is irrelevant to this piece, but the effect of such structures on the rate of military development is important.

In the United States, already noted as an important innovator, there were increased demands for accountability from the 1960s onwards for "scientific" methods such as the Program-Planning-Budgeting System (PPBS).[137] This has required greater scrutiny, study, and monitoring of proposals, in the hopes that the end result will be more cost effective; there has been a focus on the efficiency of the procurement process that has perhaps superceded focus on the effectiveness of the final product. At the same time, however, the size of the defense bureaucracy has grown, partly as a result of the need for more personnel to undertake the myriad new tasks required by these new procurement processes.[138] The complexity of the system has increased by the involvement of the services and Congress as well; this has created a "second Pentagon" of elected representatives, Army, Navy, Air Force, and civilian officials,[139] not to mention industry stakeholders, each with their own interests and desires.[140] The elected representatives of Congress have often micromanaged budget items, focusing on cost rather than strategy.[141] The services, in turn, have often fought to establish their own influence in the process, often trying to take away the central power of the Secretary of Defense.[142] Lower levels of the bureaucracy have subverted attempts by senior officials to implement unwanted reforms.[143] Often, bureaucratic actors have been content with stasis, preferring to protect their own turf rather than embrace risk.[144] This "safety first" attitude has been furthered by the funding system, which has demanded the production of three years of budgets at a time.[145] In response, groups within defense have resorted to satisficing in order to retain some day-to-day stability, rather than worry about long-term issues.[146] Narrow interest groups have dominated acquisition plans, believing that budget growth will solve all defense problems.[147] These interest groups have usually been service-based, leading to accusations by some that the uniformed military had too much influence at the highest levels of policymaking.[148]

Over 40 years ago, Samuel P. Huntington wrote a scathing critique of U.S. defense policy, terming it government by committee.[149] More contemporary analyses suggest his analysis retains validity, bar one major change: the problems he identified have become worse.[150] Huntington noted that defense programs were the products of controversy, negotiations, and bargaining between different groups. Logrolling prevails, overall objectives are lost in the interests of satisficing, and the premium is agreement and consensus, rather than a firm decision.[151] Nobody loses, but nobody truly gains. The end result is policy equilibrium, rather than radical change. This, in turn, favours the retention of traditional military systems and programs, rather than rapid evolution and progress. If that was the case in the 1950s and 1960s, when the American policy ecosystem was much smaller, then its impact today can well be imagined.

It is more difficult to examine Russian military bureaucracy during the Cold War period, but in the period since some observations can be made.[152] For the most part, military personnel have been the primary source of defense policy advice.[153] While they have espoused reform programs, they have been slow to do so. There has been limited political leadership committed to change. The bureaucracy has in turn done what most bureaucracies do when left to their own devices; it has focused on turf protection, and by extension, stasis, or at most only incremental change.

A third government worth briefly examining is that of the United Kingdom. Its procurement processes slowed down markedly during the post-World War II period, though this has been blamed on the retention of older, simpler procurement processes, which have been seen as lacking in utility when used for modern, highly complex programs.[154] The same issues of scrutiny, study, monitoring, approval, and submission have been seen to provide security for public funds but also to delay the process.[155] The United Kingdom has also been heavily engaged in multinational defense programs, which further complicate the cultural and bureaucratic issues involved and further slow down the procurement process.[156]

At the same time, the companies that produce weapons have also grown, which has had similar effects. Several mega-corporations have emerged, which are not necessarily as responsive to demands as smaller companies might be, as evidenced by NAA in the P-51 program. Many of these mergers have been linked to the end of the Cold War. Cuts in defense expenditures threatened to bankrupt weapons companies, and they in turn were forced to conglomerate. American aircraft manufacturers were especially hard hit. A large number of companies—North American,[157] Northrop,[158] Grumman, McDonnell Douglas,[159] Vought, Fairchild,[160] Martin,[161] General Dynamics,[162] Boeing,[163] and Lockheed,[164]—have merged into three mega-companies—Boeing, Lockheed-Martin, and Northrop-Grumman.

Governments, and by extension, procurement bureaucracies, have swollen in the past 50 years, lengthening development processes; since the Cold War ended, a combination of declining threat and large bureaucracies has slowed down the pace of military evolution even more. Bureaucracies require substantial push by political leadership to innovate; in the absence of a major threat, political leaderships have not seen the need for such a push, and instead bureaucracies have settled into holding patterns for the most part, progressing weapons systems conceptualized years or even decades before, focusing on maintaining existing capability within restricted funding, and in some cases carrying out urgent operational replacement of in-service equipment. It is the same with defense industry, which does not see—at least in the field of major platforms—any need to innovate and develop advanced concepts independently. In the past, major defense companies on their own initiative have funded projects such as the Northrop F-5[165] and McDonnell Douglas F-4,[166] hoping that a government would then enunciate a need for such a capability. Such financially risky behaviour seldom, if ever, occurs today, largely due to the issue of military inflation.

Defense budgets around the world have generally increased in raw terms since the end of World War II, albeit with brief downward curves during the peace dividend period of the early post-Cold War era. Since 2000, however, defense funding has tracked upwards in the major innovating countries, including the United States, Russia, and the United Kingdom. If the price of military equipment, measured per "capability unit," had stayed the same, then military evolution would have occurred at the same rate or even accelerated in recent times due to the increase in raw money.[167] Partly, this has not occurred because funding has gone to other elements of the military budget than research and development.[168] More important, however, is inflation.[169]

As development timelines have lengthened, the costs of military equipment have skyrocketed in a manner that is disproportional to their performance and disproportional to inflation in other areas of the economy.[170] This can be partly explained by the "80:20" rule, which states that for any given item of military equipment, an item with 80 percent of the capability of the best item can be obtained for 20 percent of the cost of that item; it is the final 20 percent of capability, the leading-edge and innovative aspect, that inflates the cost.[171] Estimates of the level of inflation of military equipment, while high, may only constitute a "lower bound on the true cost."[172]

Several reasons for this disproportional inflation have been posited. One is that rapid military buildups during wars causes price increases, which is not countered by deflation after the conflict due to political factors.[173] Another issue is dependence on rare materials, which can cause shortfalls and thus price increases.[174]

The cost of military systems often rises substantially over their production lifetime.[175] Partly, this is a self-sustaining issue; as costs rise, production runs are cut short, which in turn increases the per-unit cost, reducing the production run further in some cases. This has best been exemplified by American practice through the 1990s/2000s, when major programs were reduced to save costs, driving up the price of individual items and in some cases not affecting the total program cost.[176]

Other issues—the complexity of modern systems, the profit-driven interests of primary manufacturers, and wage costs—also factor into overall inflation.[177] It has been estimated that a premium of as much as 38 percent may apply for military equipment compared to its civilian counterparts.[178]

Increasing costs further slows development, as militaries, rather than focus on leading edge (and by definition) expensive technology, focus on proven, older systems for a much lower cost. The sheer cost of next-generation systems reduces demand for them, which has the follow-on effect of reducing the research and trial work required to get them into service, delaying production.

Fiscal risk aversion has been paralleled by technical risk aversion. When the United States acquired the F-104, it gained a quantum leap in capability, but also gained an aircraft that was a menace to its crews and was nicknamed *The Widow Maker* after a series of highly publicized accidents.[179] Today, as part of the Revolution in Attitudes to the Military (RAM), further examined later,[180] the public is far less willing to see military personnel perish through the operation of high-performance, but risky, equipment; indeed, they are increasingly wary of sustaining casualties on operations as well.[181] Safety requirements have become increasingly important; one only needs to consider that as recently as the 1950s, military personnel were deliberately exposed to nuclear radiation as part of experimental programs.

Cause Three: Technology Issues.

The issues of threat and culture explain much of *relative military stasis*, but it is also essential to examine issues of technology, especially complexity and related cost inflation, and the issue of scientific limits. The F/A-22, F-35, Littoral Combat Ship, and other modern systems consist of a variety of rare and exotic materials, myriad pieces, much electrical and electronic cabling, and their components are generally produced by a very large number of subcontractors.[182] However, this issue of complexity seems somewhat problematic as an explanation when it is viewed in historical context, because recent increases in complexity are not necessarily greater than those of the past.

Indeed, past technological advancements might be perceived as even greater proportional leaps in complexity than the F/A-22 over the F-15 or the F-35 over the F-16. In the 19th century, navies moved from wooden, wind-powered ships to iron-hulled, steam-powered ships in the space of a couple of decades. This was a quantum jump in complexity, involving entirely new materials and processes, demanding entirely new methods of fabrication and handling. What is more, it was done with the tools of the time, which were much less sophisticated than modern equipment. In the 1930s, airframes went from strutted and braced fabric-covered shapes to stressed-skin types, again requiring entirely new methods of production. A few years later, aircraft designers and manufacturers managed to integrate an entirely new propulsion system, the jet engine, as well as emerging electronics technology, into airframes of new design. And as the above summary showed, this leap in complexity was achieved rapidly; think of the Me-262, with swept wings, jet engines, and radar in some variants, flying in 1945, barely a decade after the P-26 entered service. A final example of a major increase in complexity is the addition of electrical wiring to warships from the early part of the 20th century. If measured by the ad-hoc variable of "fiddliness," then few other developments in military history can rival it; it involved work over the entire length and breadth of a warship, necessitating redesign or work in nearly every location. Today's modern weapons systems are no more complex than their predecessors, than Victorian-era ironclads were over their predecessors, or the F-86 was over the P-51; if anything, the difference in complexity is less. And it is difference in complexity that should matter in production times, rather than overall complexity.

Even if modern systems were an unprecedented leap in complexity, the fact is that contemporary production facilities are much more capable and sophisticated than those of the past. Computer aided design (CAD) makes blueprinting much easier, and robotic machinery and lasers now cut the parts that once required careful hand milling.[183] Manufacturing facilities are sterile to avoid contamination and resultant problems with precision items. And yet, despite these gains in production technology, military development has slowed.[184]

The key issue may not be the sheer number of components, but rather the fact that as the number of components rises, the number of interrelationships rises at a greater than linear rate.[185] An item with two components has one relationship; an item with four has six, and an item with 6 has 15. Every relationship is a potential point of failure, and thus increasing complexity results in increasing technical risk. Depending on the degree of redundancy within a system, the failure of any one of those relationships could delay the development of the total system. And, as acquisition agencies have become more risk-averse, as has been discussed earlier, they have taken longer to work through issues, rather than develop systems rapidly and accept problems, as was done with the F-104. More damagingly, there is sometimes a tendency to equate increasing technological complexity (measured by number of parts) with increased capability; the two are not synonymous.

Another issue with complexity may be that the complexity of contemporary systems has not outrun production processes, but rather the ability of the human mind, in researchers and policymakers, to understand.[186] The people today who attempt to scope military systems requirements have no greater cognitive capacity than those who scoped military systems requirements 50 or 100 years ago; if there is a gap between human capacity and technological complexity, then delays in achieving understanding are certain.

Complexity is inherently linked to a second technological issue, which will be termed "scientific limit." It is not an entirely satisfactory title, but it is the best of a bad lot. It may well be that, given our current scientific knowledge and equipment, we are simply much closer to our limits in particular fields of military technology, such as engine power, aerodynamics, firepower, and armor, than we are in other fields, such as electronics and computers. To understand this, it helps to visualise a set of circles; these stand for the boundaries of scientific, or pure, knowledge. Within these circles is shading; this stands for the degree of applied technology available in that field. When a circle is fully shaded, applied technology has reached the boundaries of scientific knowledge. When a circle is empty, applied technology has not even engaged with that field of scientific knowledge.

With certain performance criteria, such as aircraft speed, improvement may require substantial work in multiple fields of technology; for example, aerodynamics, engine power, and the weight and heat resistance of construction materials. As one approaches the limits of knowledge in certain fields, the degree of work required to attain performance gains becomes almost asymptotic. Often, knowledge in one of the required fields is lacking. For example, we might have the engines to build a mach-5 fighter, as well as the aerodynamic knowledge, but we lack the knowledge of composite materials to build one that flies. At some stage, we may reach the limits of an entire type of material or design, and be forced to develop an entirely innovative successor, rather than incrementally advance what already exists. For example, biplanes reached their zenith in the early 1930s, rifled tank guns in the 1960s, and crossbows in the 15th century. They were replaced by new systems: the stressed skin monoplane; the smoothbore cannon; and the firearm, but developing these entirely new designs may take substantial time. And, if scientific knowledge at the point at which a certain design reaches performance exhaustion does not extend to knowledge of a successor, then stasis results.

Another useful analogy can be provided here in relation to scientific limits: the fruit tree. This tree bears fruit at different levels; these are technological advances. The initial gains involve the picking of the lowest hanging fruit. After a time, what remains are the high hanging fruit: the most difficult technical problems. Getting to those fruit, and solving those problems, requires substantial effort, and it may indeed not be worthwhile to do so, if the benefits of that effort are not regarded as sufficient. It is partly because of this phenomenon that the 80:20 rule exists, as it is the difficult problems requiring the most work (and thus cost) that provide the final element of performance.

Land vehicles, in particular, present firm indicators of having reached certain physical-scientific limits. Through the 1950s, 1960s, 1970s, and 1980s, main battle tank (MBT) armor protection steadily improved in quality, with composite materials, depleted uranium liners, spall liners, and ERA entering production. Weight sometimes increased, but not in proportion to the increased protection, and sometimes more could be obtained for less: for example, a 41,000kg T-72 had substantially more protection than a 56,000kg World War II *Tiger I*. In lighter-weight vehicles (under 30,000kg), by comparison, protection increased to a lesser extent. Because of issues of volume and total surface area, the weight/protection curve favours denser, and thus heavier, vehicles disproportionately; a 40,000kg vehicle is likely to be more than twice as heavily armored as a 20,000 kg vehicle. The following shows an approximation of this relationship.

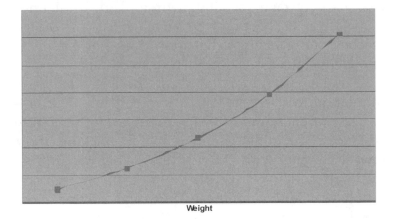

Weight

Figure 2. Weight/Protection Curve.

Massive armor simply cannot be made light enough to provide sufficient protection against likely threats; some vehicles weighing close to 20 tons are not even proof against 14.5mm fire.[187] Substantial efforts have been made to protect light vehicles, for example through ERA, slat armor, active protection systems, and other add-on packages.[188] The effect, however, is limited. Simply put, modern scientific knowledge cannot create an armor package for light vehicles that is strong enough to withstand sufficient threats: materials technology has reached its current limits. For evolution to occur, major advances in physical scientific knowledge are required to develop new materials that offer double, triple, or even more protection for the same weight or thickness. Yet nothing of the same order of magnitude of Chobham armor seems to be likely in the near future.

Scientific knowledge is advanced through research, both pure and applied, and research in fields related to military technology has declined in the post-Cold War period. Less funding has been provided, and more forces have switched to purchasing proven systems. The scientific lead has in turn been taken by commercial scientific research, which obviously has rather different priorities, and which has seen its most spectacular advances in the field of information technology. Computers today are what aircraft or tanks were in World War II; constantly improving, with new generations emerging each year, rendering previous technology obsolescent. As noted earlier, military development has followed in the wake of commercial information technology (IT), making rapid gains. And it is interesting to note that many of the major problems encountered in procurement programs in recent times have been in data networking or other computing applications:[189] the same riskiness that was once a factor in aircraft or tank development is now apparent in computer development, showing that this is indeed the "bleeding edge" of technology.

It is likely that military information technology development will continue at a rapid rate into the near future, but there are some concerns on the horizon. Miniaturization and heat dispersal issues are already threatening the further development of commercial microchips, and there are some fears that without new physical technology, performance increases will slow. However, military IT lags behind commercial development, so it will be some years before military computing encounters the same sorts of problems. By then, it is possible that commercial research will have overcome the physical issues and continued on.

CRITICIZING RELATIVE MILITARY STASIS

The final issue to discuss in relation to *relative military stasis* is to examine whether it is an entirely flawed conclusion reached by studying incorrect data. After all, how could so many commentators be wrong when they claim the military environment is evolving at a rapid rate? Criticism of the above analysis might say that the criteria used to judge military development, namely fighters, tanks, and cruisers, are simply the wrong criteria. It might be said that using them displays techno-fetishism and a bias for large platform capabilities, capabilities suited to the Cold War but not necessarily useful in our chaotic contemporary environment; as such it is eminently understandable that their development has slowed since the end of the Cold War, with military progress switching to other systems better suited to the contemporary ecosystem.[190] Measuring recent military development with those criteria would be akin to measuring the development of transport technology in the 20th century by studying the evolution of horse carriages during that period and likely to come up with the same result. Instead, one should study military progress in other fields, such as stealthiness, communications, and computing power.

There is no doubt that in certain narrow fields of military technology, especially those in which the United States, in particular, has an urgent operational need, there is hasty development. Mine resistant vehicles (MRVs), for example, are undergoing rapid evolution enabled by a streamlined research, development, and procurement process that has been specifically developed to ensure that they enter service as quickly as possible.[191] The range of Unmanned Aerial Vehicles (UAVs), which fought their first war in 1991, has exploded; there is now a plethora of types spanning the operational spectrum from "over the hill" squad-level reconnaissance to long endurance strategic surveillance.[192] Robotic ground vehicles are become steadily more advanced with each successive generation, and the time lag between generations is short. Were we to use those systems as our criteria for measuring military progress, we might come to quite a different conclusion, and suggest that we are in a time of rapid military evolution.

This is a tenuous assertion for several reasons. First, those capabilities that have seen substantial development in recent times are niche capabilities that occupy only a very small part of military organizations; they are not the cornerstones around which air forces, armies, and navies are built. They are far outnumbered by other projects in which development is much slower, and in which old technology continues to serve, albeit upgraded.

Second, if those are the important capabilities today, why are militaries around the world still developing, albeit slowly, the types of weapons systems—fighters, tanks, and warships—that were used for the analysis of this article? The United States is producing the Joint Strike Fighter (JSF), Future Combat System (FCS), and Littoral Combat Ship (LCS). Russia is developing advanced versions of its *Sukhoi* and *MiG* fighters, as well as upgrading its tank fleet. The United Kingdom and other European states have recently produced the *Eurofighter*. It appears that militaries still feel that major platforms have utility in the contemporary and future strategic environment; if that is so, then surely they are valid criteria for measurement.[193]

Third, there is the counterfactual argument of whether or not development today is more rapid than might have been the case otherwise. Had the Cold War not ended, it is likely that the development of UAVs and robotic ground vehicles would have occurred at a similar, if not quicker rate; after all, they were initially designed for the superpower confrontation, and we have evidence in other fields, such as fighter aircraft, as to just how swiftly development can occur when confronted with such an environment. This line of argument suggests that while progress may seem rapid, it only seems so because we lack context; first, we cannot tell what might have happened otherwise; second, because the systems are new, we cannot measure their recent evolution against their historical evolution; and thirdly, because other systems are developing so slowly today, we cannot truly judge the rate at which these niche capabilities are developing: they seem fast, but it is only a comparative measure.

A final reason that this assertion is tenuous is that the rapid evolution in certain systems it describes has taken place only in the past 2 to 3 years; it is, at best, an anomaly amidst the general trend of slowing development that has dominated the past 2 decades.

Overall, the argument that we are not in a period of *relative military stasis* appears to be flawed. Development in a few niche capabilities does not indicate overall development; progress in large, high-capability systems, which make up the majority of military technological development, has slowed. This criticism does, however, suggest that we should consider the possibility that we are in the midst of a transition to a new military paradigm, where those traditional systems we have analysed are becoming, or will become, less relevant, although they retain relevance today. This then leads us, after some delay, into a discussion of the Revolution in Military Affairs, or RMA.

THE REVOLUTION IN MILITARY AFFAIRS

While much of the RMA is implicit, or briefly mentioned, in the above sections, it has been a deliberate choice not to focus too strongly on it until now, lest it color the analysis by presupposing a conclusion that, at heart, is diametrically opposed to the findings of this work. At its core, the RMA suggests that through the networking and integration of sensors and shooters, a process often called transformation, revolutionary new gains in military effectiveness can be achieved.[194] The first real thinking on this matter took place in the late 1980s in the Soviet Union, when Marshal Ogarkov predicted that developing U.S. capabilities portended what he called a Military Technical Revolution (MTR).[195] The Gulf War of 1990-91 seemed to bear out his thinking, as U.S. forces operating in a semi-transformed fashion very rapidly defeated a numerically large and adequately equipped force with minimal casualties. The RMA thus became a favoured topic for military thought through much of the 1990s.[196] Some of the more ardent advocates of the RMA felt that it portended the end of the "fog of war" and the possibility that commanders could have full situational awareness of the battlespace.[197] The end of the linear battlefield was predicted, to be replaced by a three-dimensional battlespace filled with modular units. Ever more radical concepts of operations, such as swarming, were propounded as well.[198] A change in military operations of as great a magnitude as the switch to metal weapons, firearms, and blitzkrieg, was predicted.

If there has indeed been an RMA in the past 15 years, then it seems absurd—if not impossible—to suggest that we are in a period of *relative military stasis*. However, it is possible that the two could co-exist. An RMA represents the culmination of a series of technological trends and their reaching critical mass.[199] It does not require substantial technological progress in any specific field (although it can be created through such progress, as with firearms); rather, it is in the interactions between systems, for example through data networks, that a revolutionary military capability is achieved.[200] The blitzkrieg RMA was carried out by enabling technologies—tanks, radios, close air support—that had individually been around for some time.[201] What occurred, however, was that they achieved a level of technological maturity sufficient to enable their integration into a common force, as well as assure operational reliability of a level to sustain advances; there is no value in a powerful system that never works. This combination was thus more than merely the sum of its parts. Also essential was the development of concepts and doctrine necessary for optimal usage; mental evolution was as critical as the development of radios. One could integrate the themes of *relative military stasis* and the RMA by suggesting that the technologies that might enable a contemporary RMA were, by and large, developed during the Cold War period, and that the RMA was enabled by, say, 1991 or so; all that has occurred since then has been slow and steady development past the point of critical mass.

Occam's razor, however, suggests a much simpler way to deal with the issue of the RMA: to question whether an RMA even exists.[202] There are strong arguments against the existence of an RMA. An RMA requires militaries to transform, to adapt their organizational structures, doctrine, and technology to operate in revolutionary fashion. Anything less, by definition, is not an RMA, which occasionally appears to be ignored by those who would see in substantial enhancement and evolution in technology or capability the equivalent of an RMA. An RMA cannot occur if it exists only on paper or in the mind. Given that, it appears that insufficient militaries have transformed for an RMA to have occurred. The most transformational military in the world, the United States, is still far from having the sort of futuristic capabilities espoused by RMA proponents through the 1990s.[203] Other militaries, even those as advanced as the British, German, Russian, and Israeli, have transformed even less.

There are good reasons why the current RMA has not yet been realized. The first is cost. It is extremely expensive to develop, acquire, and integrate the sorts of high technology communications and weapons systems required to transform capability. Doing so, given a fixed pool of funding, must limit expenditure in other areas, such as wages, training, and exercises. In particular, going down the transformed route will usually mean there is less money for personnel, and so soldier numbers decline. This, in turn, has implications for the second issue about the RMA, and that is its applicability.

RMA transformational concepts of operations seem to have limited applicability across the full spectrum of operations.[204] Operation ALLIED FORCE in 1999 involved a North Atlantic Treaty Organization (NATO) air campaign against Serbia. NATO could bring to bear a massive amount of precision guided aerial firepower against a much lower technology opponent; despite this, it still took 3 months before Serbia gave in.[205] In 2003, a partially transformed U.S. force conquered Iraq in several weeks, winning the conventional battle with little cost.[206] In the 5 years since, that same force has proven unable to defeat a tenacious insurgency.[207] Transformed militaries are not silver bullets; the uncertainty of warfare precludes any scientific or linear solution to battle.[208] War is not operational analysis. Counterinsurgencies, peace support operations, humanitarian interventions, and anti-terrorist deployments are just some of the types of military operation that do not seem to lend themselves easily to RMA concepts of operations.[209] This is mainly because of the cost related issues noted above — transformed militaries have fewer personnel and fewer items of equipment, and quantity has a quality all its own.[210]

Transformed militaries also have vulnerabilities absent from more traditional structures. Their heavy reliance on data communications and electronics opens them to a range of specialist attacks, ranging from electro-magnetic pulses (EMP) to the cutting of power lines; a force that relies on electronics may fail if those electronic links disappear.

Overall, then, while weapons systems are more accurate, more interlinked with command and sensor nodes, more responsive, and potentially more effective, there has not been an RMA; not if an RMA means a major shift in the nature of warfare. There has instead been an EMA: Evolution in Military Affairs. The fact that an RMA has not occurred, despite being prophesied some 20 years ago, might be regarded as further proof of the central thesis of this work. Had technological advancement progressed at the same rate during that time as it did during the 1950s or 1960s, then there seems little doubt that the RMA would have been fulfilled by today. We would today see fully or mostly transformed militaries, rather than the hodgepodge of new and legacy systems that exists instead.

BROADER ISSUES OF THE STRATEGIC ENVIRONMENT

However, technology is only half the story when it comes to the contemporary strategic environment. Focus is now shifted from technology to a range of broader issues, including the nature of conflict. Again, from reading a wide range of commentators and analysts,[211] it seems that surely the strategic environment is in a period of chaos and rapid change.[212] We are in a period of "fourth generation warfare."[213] Soldiers must fight the "three-block war," carrying out "complex maneuver."[214] Primordial ethnic hatred is enabled by modern technology; vicious murderers carry state of the art cellphones and high-powered rifles. At the same time, mass-casualty terrorist attacks are carried out by religious fanatics wielding box-cutter blades. As was briefly noted at the start of this article, the world may no longer rest under a nuclear Sword of Damocles, but it is certainly not a particularly peaceful place; though threat and danger has reduced, they are still an essential part of the environment.

Western militaries are constantly in action,[215] keeping the peace, fighting insurgencies, or merely providing food aid. Analysts talk about this environment in disheartening terms. It is seen as a new era of conflict, one that is clearly distinct from the Cold War, where even if we faced destruction, at least the battle lines were clearly drawn, the sides were easily distinguished, and the threat could be counted, tabulated, and countered.[216] These assertions are partly true. The post-Cold War era is different from the Cold War era. However, it does not necessarily follow that the post-Cold War era is entirely novel, nor does it necessarily follow that there is nothing in common between the Cold War and post-Cold War eras.

A key issue here is that the Cold War, which was a period of relative strategic simplicity when strategic perceptions focused on bipolar confrontation and large scale war, was a historical anomaly. However, for whatever reasons, commentators, policymakers, and analysts have committed a modified form of distorted presentism in assuming that the Cold War was militarily normal. This flawed perception then leads into a belief that it is military normal for the strategic environment to feature state-controlled, uniformed actors, whose likely role will be major conventional or nuclear warfare, and whose functions are clearly distinct from those of the police and other security agencies.[217] Extensions of this belief include the commonly held attitudes that peacekeeping is not a fitting role for militaries, that counterinsurgency is largely a waste of time, that the military should not play a part in domestic security and politics, and that religion and ethnicity are not valid aspects of conflict. It is a firmly Western-culturally-centric attitude (and by Western, I include modernized states around the world, including the former Warsaw Pact and countries such as Japan), and one that, when assessed against the broad scope of military history, seems rather anomalous.[218]

When we look at the broad swathe of military history, the stories and tales of warriors, soldiers, war bands, and armies, it becomes swiftly apparent that conventional, open, decisive warfare is actually a relatively rare occurrence. Roman soldiers, who controlled one of the world's greatest empires, functioned as police, as customs officials, as anti-piracy patrollers, and as hunters of insurgents. They built roads and towns, assisted in the rise — and fall —

of Caesars, and helped spread, or limit the spread of, religions across the breadth of the empire, from Mithras through to Christianity. The British in the 18th and 19th centuries, who ruled over the world's largest empire when measured in total geographical extent, had regular soldiers trained in drill for the battlefields of Europe, but who, by and large, were involved in small wars.[219] They battled native contingents in platoon level engagements from Afghanistan to New Zealand to Africa. They policed borders and towns and helped push railroads into the depths of India. Redcoats fought Native Americans who had bows and arrows, as well as Napoleon's Guards who had muskets and cannon. The Royal Navy participated as well, destroying slavers along the African coast, shipping convicts to Australia, forcing opium into China, and keeping a line of "weatherbeat'n ships" against the French.

Socrates, who was mentioned earlier discoursing on youth, was not merely a philosopher. He was also a soldier for a time. At the battle of Potidaea, when the Athenian forces had been defeated, he took firm control of a small group of phalangites as they retreated, and in doing so averted a likely massacre.[220] The Anglo-Saxons who invaded England were farmers first, warriors second; they took up their seaxes to gain more land for their scythes.[221] The Normans who followed them would likely be called transnational criminals today. From their Scandinavian bases, they sailed, ripping out enclaves in Sicily, mainland Italy, and France, destroying local governments, and taking land and power;[222] they were little different from many contemporary and recent African warlords. Their soldiers forced an entirely new language and legal system upon England, and when the situation had calmed down, the most elite of their troops—the knights—spent much of their time engaged in jousts, wargames in modern parlance, rather than military engagements. They also managed to develop a complex system of etiquette known as chivalry, which affects our moral standards even today.

The simplicity of a clear distinction between sides was also one often lacking from the historical story. Races, nationalities, and religions were divided. There were complex webs of deceit and betrayal; many a battle was decided by the sudden treachery of a disloyal duke or earl. When Alexander the Great launched his crusade upon the Persian Empire, ostensibly to avenge injuries done to the Greeks by the Persians at Plataea and other battles and to extend Greek culture and power, the most potent of his foes were mercenary Greek phalangites.[223] Those Greeks valued gold over ethnic and cultural loyalties. As Alexander marched further east, he himself incorporated Persian elements into his force, stimulating revolt among his soldiers and bringing some to wonder whether his motives had changed and whether he had "gone native."

In the 12th century, the Pope called for the First Crusade, largely to respond to appeals by Byzantium. That nation, the remnant of the Eastern Roman Empire, had for many years been subject to the depredations of the Arabs, newly converted to Islam. A century later, another Crusade was called, and largely Latin Crusaders marched east to defend Christianity and retake the Holy Land. Their route took them past Byzantium, the same city that had launched their quest so many years before. But now, as the Latins camped before the walls of the city known as the "Jewel of the East," they were seized with a desire far more base than religious duty and defense of the faith: a desire to seize the wealth of the city. A labyrinthine series of plot and counterplot followed, and eventually the Crusaders entered and sacked the city.[224] Complexity, and the intermingling of ethnicity, religion, and greed, is not a merely modern phenomenon.

A third example further illustrates the point. The Mamelukes of the Turkish Empire were descended from a horse people of the Central Asian steppe, enslaved and taken into service by what was a more advanced state. When the Mongols of Genghis Khan swept across Asia and the Near East, they seemed unstoppable; the entire world trembled at their coming. Yet, at Ain Jalut, the Mamelukes met and stopped the Mongols.[225] One horse people defeated another; though their cultures were, at heart, the same, they found themselves on opposite sides. One served an organized state, and the other sought merely to conquer, despoil, and destroy. That type of conflict, then, is not one that has only emerged in recent times.

Building from the observation that the Cold War's simplicity was anomalous in historical context, we can then state that the return to complexity since is a return to military normality. Yet, it might also be noted that the Cold War was not as simple as it is often perceived, and there are elements of continuity with the post-Cold War period.

It is easy to perceive the Cold War as a period of relative peace, secured by deterrence and bipolar rivalry. A closer look, however, shows that in some aspects this perception is flawed. There were many hot wars during the Cold War, and some two-thirds of them were internal rather than interstate conflicts.[226] There were complex peace operations in the Congo;[227] there were preemptive strikes against potential weapons of mass destruction (WMD) facilities, such as that carried out by Israel against Iraq; and there were forcible humanitarian interventions. Much of the complexity of the Cold War came from proxy conflicts sponsored by the superpowers.

SEPARATING THE COLD WAR AND POST-COLD WAR PERIODS

The key separation between the Cold War and post-Cold War periods is attitude. Militaries, especially Western militaries, were constrained by the demands of superpower rivalry during the Cold War period. The stakes were too high to allow any wasted effort, and as such, militaries were focused on the demands of conventional and nuclear war, even though such operations seldom, or never, occurred. If inter-bloc war had erupted, it would have required all the military resources of the combatant nations; they needed to keep their powder dry. Peace operations, ethnic conflicts, humanitarian crises all occurred, and occurred quite often, but they were regarded as being of secondary or even tertiary importance: sideshows. The simplicity of the Cold War was thus partially a case of tunnel vision, which caused policymakers and analysts to focus only on the greatest threat. Considering the destruction that World War III might have caused, that tunnel vision was entirely legitimate.

Attitudes have since changed. The Cold War thawed out, as has been noted earlier. With the disappearance of the major threat, the perceptions of militaries around the world changed. They began to more clearly notice all of the other types of conflict and crisis that they had deliberately ignored for almost half a century. They began to worry that unless they could find other tasks to undertake, separate from major war, they would become obsolescent, and be reduced or even disbanded; to borrow an analogy from civil employment, they faced looming redundancy. In the case of major alliances, some have disappeared, such as the Warsaw Pact, and others have been forced to reinvent themselves in order to survive a changing environment, such as NATO.[228] At the same time, there seems to have been a tendency to gild the truffle, to regard the post-Cold War and post-September 11, 2001 (9/11) eras as something new, unique, innovative, chaotic, and somehow very different to anything that has gone before.[229]

The post-Cold War strategic environment has been characterized by six (and one) major themes.[230] The first of these is amorphous, and has a broad influence over the other themes. It is hard to name, but terming it "globalization and the new world order" seems the most accurate. It is a multifaceted concept, but it might best be perceived as the way in which the world has become smaller and increasingly unified through the combination of technology and culture. It has had its effect on conflict, especially through its facilitation of the collision of cultural values via mass media. It has weakened interstate barriers, freeing up the movement of people, including terrorists and criminals. A decline in the value of state sovereignty has been linked to globalization. There has been a developing trend towards intervention in the internal affairs of states, often justified by appeals to "human rights."[231] Finally, the media have played an increasingly important role in shaping the post-Cold War strategic environment, largely because technology has increased the media's reach and duration.[232] They have been a cause of conflict, as in Rwanda. They have helped to shape responses to conflicts through the manipulation of public sentiment, as in Somalia. At the same time, they have restricted what militaries can do, as their activities are now under the spotlight more often. At their most extreme, the media have been a prime factor in withdrawal from an operation, as happened after the infamous Battle of Mogadishu in 1994. Representative democracies are particularly vulnerable in such cases.

The second major theme is resource and environmental pressures. During the Cold War, such issues were relegated to secondary status. In recent years, however, they have gained increased salience: by and large, problems have intensified, as most resources are fixed in quantity, and consumption continues to increase unabated. Resource shortages, or more specifically the balancing of resources between two factions, can cause conflicts, both internal and external. In Bougainville, copper mining was a major factor for conflict;[233] in the South China Sea, a supposed treasure trove of gas and oil, there has been much sabre rattling. Environmental issues also shape responses to conflict, imposing limitations on operations. Given the non-renewable nature of most resources, and that populations continue to grow, it is likely that resource issues will intensify in the future.

Ethnic conflict is the third major issue. There seems to be an intuitive link between the end of the Cold War and the rise of ethnic conflict.[234] The withdrawal of superpower influence and patronage in many areas caused a power vacuum into which other ideologies, such as hyper-nationalism and ethnic hatred, could emerge. Many central governments, suddenly bereft of the external aid given them by the United States or Soviet Union, were now unable to control their outer territories; in some cases, ethnic warlords occupied such spaces instead. When countries switched from

Communist to free market economies, there were often problems. Resultant socio-economic disparities were sometimes divided along ethnic lines, creating grievances. Simultaneously, democracy began to develop, and with it came a concomitant increase in free speech, speech often used to express inflammatory ethnic rhetoric. This combination of factors resulted in ethnic conflicts of exceeding savagery in several cases, often marked by the massacre of civilians or the use of sexual assault as a weapon of war. Combatant sides have seldom been hierarchical, disciplined forces, but have rather been coalitions of local militias, paramilitary groups, and elements of organized crime. Much of their fighting has been within cities. Overall, ethnic conflicts have proven very difficult to resolve, as the issue central to each side is often its own existence; in such cases, compromise is impossible.

The fourth major theme is the rise of terrorism. During the Cold War, terrorism was generally politico-ideological, often Marxist, and carried out to create publicity for a cause, rather than slaughter innocents.[235] Post-Cold War terrorism, in comparison, has proven to be exceedingly deadly,[236] and the number of deaths per terrorist event climbed steadily through the 1990s, peaking with the 9/11 attacks. Since then, a new era of fear and doubt about terrorism has emerged, and there have been further, major attacks in such capitals as Moscow, Madrid, and London. These attacks usually have been undertaken by religiously-motivated groups who do not share the same concern with casualties as did their politically-motivated predecessors. In some cases, religious terrorists seek their own death as well, believing it the swiftest path to reward in the afterlife. Religious terrorist groups can cloak themselves behind other radical religious groups, making identification difficult, and their goals are often extraordinarily ambitious, such as the creation of religious empires in the Middle East. Modern technology, especially cellphones and the Internet, has further enhanced the ability of terrorists to carry out devastating strikes. Luckily for the world, except for a few minor incidents, extremist terrorist groups have been unable to secure and use WMDs.

This theme of WMDs is the fifth in our discussion of post-Cold War trends. During the Cold War, most nuclear, biological, and chemical weapons were produced by "status quo" states, whose actions with such weapons could reasonably be predicted. In recent years, however, so-called "rogue states" such as North Korea and Iraq have embarked on the development of WMDs, and in the former case, have achieved a nuclear missile capability. There is also concern that WMDs might proliferate beyond state control, especially if "rogue states" provide them to terrorist groups or other violent nonstate actors.[237] This is a terrifying prospect. Nuclear weapons are unrivaled in destructive power. Biological weapons are extremely lethal, as well as being self-perpetuating. Chemical weapons can kill in microscopic doses. Were a terrorist group to acquire WMD, it would enable them to respond to the technological and size dominance of militaries in asymmetrical fashion, for example by detonating a suitcase-sized nuclear weapon in a city. However, WMDs are not simple to acquire or use. Nuclear weapons are especially difficult to fabricate, requiring precision machinery; chemical and biological weapons are more easily created, but storage and especially dispersal present serious problems. There have been a few terrorist chemical attacks, but they have been largely failures.

The sixth theme important to the post-Cold War period is the RMA, which has earlier been discussed in some detail. Even if its potentiality has not been realized, it has still shaped the strategic environment, even if only by altering the perceptions of defense policymakers around the globe.

These six main issues interrelate in complex fashion. For example, the end of the Cold War resulted in the rise of democracy in successor states, which in turn helped create ethnic conflict. Those ethnic conflicts, in turn, have proven to be breeding grounds for terrorist groups, or at least provided "lawless lands" where such groups can survive. The proliferation of WMDs and the simultaneous increase in the quantity and intensity of terrorism is another dangerous interaction. Also important is the interaction between technical and political issues; for example, the RMA, if realized, might alter the decisionmaking process of political leaders when going to war. It might also alter the global balance of power in a short period of time. Globalization alters the nature of relationships between states, other organizations, and individuals, shaping strategy and tactics.

All of these six issues are real, all affect the strategic environment, and all in one way or another are dangerous. Yet, and it may seem like flogging a dead horse, that does not necessarily make them new. The most important development in recent years has not been the emergence of these issues; it has been the disappearance of the Cold War, which has led to more attention being paid to them. Perception is key.

THE REVOLUTION IN ATTITUDES TOWARDS THE MILITARY

Perception leads into the "one" of the six (and one) noted earlier, and perhaps the one theme that is truly novel; it may well be the theme that has the greatest effect on the future shape of the strategic environment. It is closely related to both globalization and the RMA, and it is another revolution: the Revolution in Attitudes towards the Military (RAM).[238] Grossly simplified, it refers to a change in perceptions that is especially apparent in Western democracies. Populations are less willing to serve, demand greater civilian control over defense matters, and are far more casualty-averse. While there has been some alteration to those attitudes in some countries since the events of 9/11, by and large they grow continually stronger around the globe. Militaries have become more politically correct, have embraced diversity and sexual equality, and have become tagged more and more with such roles as peace operations and civil reconstruction, rather than warfighting. Support for `militaries is as high, if not higher, than was the case historically, but the character of that support has changed. Partly, the RAM has come about through the increasing reach of the media, but it is also a sign of the changing political maturity of electorates around the world. Without the overarching threat of the Cold War, the public seldom sees a military cause worth dying or killing for in any great numbers. At the same time, they are wary of the limitations that the high cost of military acquisitions impose on other domestic spending programs.

The future is likely to involve the continuation of these post-Cold War trends. There will be no one type of war;[239] it is likely to be land-based, intrastate, small in scale, and heavily influenced by domestic demands, but that cannot be assured. There may be an odd juxtaposition of primordial, ethnic forces equipped with lightweight, high-technology weapons.

Is this future, to return to our central question, new, innovative, unique? It is not. Conventional warfare has never been particularly common. State-on-state warfare has also been a historical rarity. The vast majority of conflicts have been small-scale; the world wars are named such because they were anomalies, not because they were usual. Land forces have also been the decisive arm for as long as war has occurred; most naval battles of great importance have been linked to land campaigns, and air forces are not even a century old. Our environment is not one of radical change, of "next generation warfare"; it is a return to military normalcy after the anomaly of the Cold War (and, by extension, the anomalies of World Wars I and II, and the world embracement of Clausewitz). What this conclusion means to the world is unclear to the author. At its least, it is a firm reinforcement to us that we should endeavour to ensure that the emperor is indeed wearing new finery. Strategic thought, like haute couture, has its fashions and its trends; it was Clausewitz once, then when the United States began its shift towards maneuver in the 1970s, it was the German writers; in the 1990s and 2000s, it has often been Sun Tzu. The fashion recently has been to believe that our contemporary environment is chaotic, unique, and fast-moving; the evidence suggests the opposite in several areas. The question is why this particular construction of the strategic environment has become accepted. In answer to this, it seems to the author that those with authority in the field also have a vested interest in portraying the environment as chaotic and rapidly changing.

NEED FOR FURTHER ANALYSIS

What is needed, however, is further study. This article is too brief to fully engage with many of the issues it covers, and many of its arguments and conclusions are open to substantial criticism and correction. Rather than propose policy changes, then, this article proposes a range of studies that could be carried out to ensure that we truly understand the character of the strategic environment.

An important study would be to identify other criteria that can be used to judge military progress. Another might examine dates in closer detail, identifying the point(s) at which technological development truly began to slow. Such a study would in itself suggest the need for thought being put into what definition of analysis is required. If one accepts the central thesis of *relative military stasis*, then it seems clear the further investigation into the causes of this stasis would be warranted. What causes hyperinflation? How does complexity interact with development times? Are effectiveness and efficiency mutually contradictory? Could an extremely high-definition analysis of the man-hours bill of various programs be done?

At higher levels, further attention might be paid to comparing Cold War and post-Cold War issues. This would then lead into a discussion of the effect of certain types of operations on military technological progress; do low intensity operations slow evolution? And, from that, when does an evolution become a revolution? Why did the RMA not catch on? Why do we want to perceive the world as changing? Was the Cold War as monolithic as it appears — perhaps the level of fear and threat did decline over time and this may be a simple explanation for slowing development times. There are many avenues for further study, and it is the earnest hope of this writer that at least some of them will be explored by others, even if only for the purpose of demolishing the tenets of this monograph.

CONCLUSION

This monograph began by looking at the development of military technology in recent years. It looked at three major platforms: fighter aircraft, tanks, and cruisers, examining the gaps between generations as well as the capability gains of each succeeding type. What it showed, quite clearly, was that development has slowed, but at the same time capability increases have also slowed: it takes longer to get new equipment, and that new equipment is less of an improvement over its predecessor than its predecessor was over its predecessor. It is thus a period of declining gains. Only in electronics and computer technology was that thesis shown to be somewhat untrue, but even there military technology has lagged significantly behind commercial advances, and thus to call it innovative and rapidly developing is to draw a long bow. This *relative military stasis*, in technology, at least, has a range of causes: the end of the Cold War, bureaucratic changes, political cultures, scientific limits, cost inflation, a focus on new characteristics that cannot be so easily measured. The monograph then looked at the strategic environment to see whether that has evolved rapidly while technology has proven more dormant. It noted that many of the issues that characterize the post-Cold War period were also present during the

Cold War; they may be newly important, but they are not necessarily new. Indeed, the contemporary period may be seen as a return to military normalcy after the lengthy anomaly of the Cold War. It is a shift away from state-on-state conflict, away from large scale war, away from a view that sees armies as forces designed solely for decisive, Clausewitzian battles. Yes, there has been change since the end of the Cold War, but it should not be exaggerated; rather than innovation, it might be taken as reaction, and we should instead examine the Cold War from a new perspective as a period of radical innovation in strategic terms, which would further be reinforced by the rapid technological development that characterized it.

Let us return to the beginning. This monograph began with an examination of the development of the F/A-22. The F/A-22 is expected to remain in service until 2050; this will be 66 years since the detailed requirements for the Advanced Tactical Fighter were set.[240] This is a long time in military history; 66 years ago, a fighter known as the P-51 was entering service. That is an argument from extremes, but it is still valid nonetheless. Today's military environment moves slowly; let us be willing to accept that, rather than assume that because it is our environment, it must somehow be more innovative than those that have gone before. Let us use the time that this relative military stasis affords us to examine the strategic environment both more closely and from a greater distance.

ENDNOTES

1. It would be impossible to make an exhaustive list of sources that state that we are in a time of rapid change, but the following provide a good start point for the interested reader. It is also not the goal of this monograph to criticize or attack particular pieces, but rather to suggest that more thought needs to be put into our characterizations of the contemporary environment. The following provide a fair introduction to many of the issues. Richard Bitzinger, *Defense Transformation and the Asia Pacific: Implications for Regional Militaries*, Honolulu, HI: Asia-Pacific Center for Strategic Studies, 2004; Jim Garamone, "Mullen Addresses Rapid Change, Other Issues at Australian War College," 2008, available from *www.defenselink.mil/news/newsarticle.aspx?id=49054*; David Lonsdale, *The Nature of War in the Information Age: Clausewitzian Future*, London: Frank Cass, 2004; Herfrieds Munkler, *The New Wars*, Cambridge: Polity, 2005; John Bennett, "Interview with James Finley," *DefenseNews*, December 17, 2007; Department of the Army, *The Strategic Environment and Army Organization*, updated June 2005, available from *www.army.mil/fm1/chapter2.html*; Williamson Murray, *The Emerging Strategic Environment: Challenges of the Twenty-First Century*, Westport, CT: Praeger Publishers, 1999; Project on Defense Alternatives, "The RMA Debate," available from *www.comw.org/rma/fulltext/overview.html*.

2. Colin Gray, *Strategy for Chaos*, London: Frank Cass, 2002; Yahya Sadowski, *The Myth of Global Chaos*, Washington DC: Brookings Institution, 1998. These two books are good start points for reading on the concept of global chaos/new world disorder.

3. John Alexander, *Winning the War: Advanced Weapons, Strategies and Concepts for the Post 9/11 World*, New York: St Martin's Press, 2003; Michael Evans, "Appointment in Samarra: Western Strategic Thought and the Culture of Risk," in Michael Evans, Alan Ryan, and Russell Parkin, eds., *Future Armies, Future Challengers: Land Warfare in the Information Age*, Crows Nest: Allen & Unwin, 2004; Michael Evans, "Clausewitz's Chameleon: Military Theory and Practice in the Early 21st Century," in Evans *et al.*, eds., *Future Armies, Future Challengers*; Lonsdale, *The Nature of War in the Information Age*; Thomas Mahnken, "The American Way of War in the Twenty-First Century," in Efraim Inbar, ed., *Democracies and Small Wars*, London: Frank Cass, 2003; Ralph

Peters, "The West's Future Foes: Simplification and Slaughter," in Evans *et al.*, eds., *Future Armies, Future Challengers*; Alan Ryan, "Land forces in 21st Century Coalition Operations: Implications for the Asia-Pacific," in Evans *et al.*, eds., *Future Armies, Future Challengers*; Raimo Vayrynen, "Capitalism, War and Peace," in Raimo Vayrynen, ed., *The Waning of Major War: Theories and Debates*, London: Routledge, 2006.

4. Simon Collins, "Being There for the Teens in Trouble," *New Zealand Herald*, February 9, 2008; Angela Gregory, "Classroom Cops Plan Raises Pupil Rights Fears," *New Zealand Herald*, February 19, 2008; "Helen Clark: State of the Nation Address," *New Zealand Herald*, January 30, 2008; "John Key: State of the Nation Speech," *New Zealand Herald*, January 30, 2008; Fran O'sullivan, "Problems Need Answers Rather than Blame Game," *New Zealand Herald*, February 2, 2008; Claire Trevett, "Opponents Tag Bill an Electioneering Stunt," *New Zealand Herald*, February 22, 2008.

5. Robin Friedman, "Youth Speak," *eJournalUSA*, August 2007, available from *usinfo.state.gov/journals/itsv/0807/ijse/friedman.htm*.

6. "Respectfully Quoted: A Dictionary of Quotations," 1989, available from *www.bartleby.com/73/195.html*.

7. *ThinkExist.com*, "Youth Quotes," available from *thinkexist. com/quotations/youth/4.html*.

8. *F22-raptor.com*, "F-22 Chronology," available from *www. f22-raptor.com/about/chronology.html*.

9. Harold Hutchison, "F-22 Struts Its Stuff," 2006, available from *www.f-16.net/news_article1916.html*.

10. "Dave's Warbirds-P-51," available from *www.daveswarbirds. com/usplanes/aircraft/mustang.htm*; "P-51 Mustang," updated November 25, 2006, available from *www.aviation-history.com*.

11. Martin van Creveld, *The Changing Face of War: Lessons of Combat, from the Marne to Iraq*, New York: Presidio Press, 2007, p. 162.

12. For reasons of length and focus, this article has had to be selective. Some systems are not covered; often, this is because they are not yet in service or it is felt that they show nothing that cannot be indicated through an examination of other systems. However, by covering three major areas over a multinational span, it is felt sufficient breadth of analysis has been achieved.

13. Lawrence Freedman, *The Cold War: A Military History*, London: Cassell, 2001; Samuel Payne Jnr, *The Conduct of War: An Introduction to Modern Warfare*, Oxford: Blackwell, 1988.

14. The following dates may not be agreed to by all, but minor variations of a year or two do not alter the overall findings of this section.

15. Robert Guttman, "Boeing P-26 Peashooter," 1996, available from *www.historynet.com/magazines/aviation_history/3030976.html? page=4&c=y*; Wings Over Arkansas, "Boeing History: P-26 'Pea-shooter' Fighter," available from *www.wingsoverkansas.com/history/ article.asp?id=760*.

16. Warbird Alley, "Curtiss P-40 Warhawk," available from *www.warbirdalley.com/p40.htm*.

17. The Military Factory, "Republic F-84 Thunderjet/ Thunderstreak/Thunderflash-World Military Aircraft," available from *www.militaryfactory.com/aircraft/detail.asp?aircraft_id=112*.

18. Warbird Alley, "North American F-86 Sabre/FJ-2/3/4 Fury," available from *www.warbirdalley.com/f86.htm*.

19. *Global Security.org*, "F-104 Starfighter," available from *www.globalsecurity.org/military/systems/aircraft/f-104-specs.htm*; Harry Luijkx, "Lockheed F-104 Starfighter Site," available from *www.starfighters.nl/*; Jirka Wagner, "Lockheed F-104 Starfighter," available from *www.military.cz/usa/air/post_war/f104/f104hist_ en.htm*.

20. *Global Security.org*, "F-4 Phantom II," available from *www. globalsecurity.org/military/systems/aircraft/f-4-history.htm*.

21. *Global Security.org*, "F-15 Eagle," available from *www. globalsecurity.org/military/systems/aircraft/f-15-history.htm*; Greg Goebel, "F-15 Origins & Variants," updated July 1, 2003, available from *www.faqs.org/docs/air/avf15_1.html*.

22. *Global Security.org*, "F-16 Fighting Falcon," available from *www.globalsecurity.org/military/systems/aircraft/f-16-history.htm*.

23. Department of the Navy-Navy Historical Center, "F/A-18 HORNET and F/A-18 SUPER HORNET," updated November 15, 2000, available from *www.history.navy.mil/planes/fa18.htm*; *Global Security.org*, "F/A-18 Hornet," available from *www.globalsecurity. org/military/systems/aircraft/f-18.htm*.

24. Guttman, "Boeing P-26 Peashooter"; Wings Over Arkansas, "Boeing History: P-26 "Peashooter" Fighter."

25. Warbird Alley, "Curtiss P-40 Warhawk."

26. The Military Factory, "Republic F-84 Thunderjet/ Thunderstreak/Thunderflash-World Military Aircraft."

27. Warbird Alley, "North American F-86 Sabre/FJ-2/3/4 Fury."

28. *Global Security.org*, "F-104 Starfighter"; Luijkx, "Lockheed F-104 Starfighter Site"; Wagner, "Lockheed F-104 Starfighter."

29. *Global Security.org*, "F-4 Phantom II."

30. *Global Security.org*, "F-15 Eagle"; *Global Security.org*, "F-15 Eagle Service Life," available from *www.globalsecurity.org/military/ systems/aircraft/f-15-life.htm*; Goebel, "F-15 Origins & Variants."

31. *Global Security.org*, "F-16 Fighting Falcon."

32. Department of the Navy-Navy Historical Center, "F/A-18 HORNET and F/A-18 SUPER HORNET"; *Global Security.org*, "F/A-18 Hornet."

33. FAS Military Analysis Network, "AIM-9 Sidewinder," updated April 23, 2000, available from *www.fas.org/man/dod-101/ sys/missile/aim-9.htm*.

34. Goebel, "F-15 Origins & Variants."

35. *Global Security.org*, "F-16 Fighting Falcon"; National Aeronautics and Space Association, "FACT SHEETS F-8 Digital Fly-By-Wire Aircraft," 2007, available from *www.nasa.gov/centers/ dryden/news/FactSheets/FS-024-DFRC.html*.

36. FAS Military Analysis Network, "F-117A Nighthawk," updated April 11, 2006, available from *www.fas.org/man/dod-101/ sys/ac/f-117.htm*.

37. This piece does not deal with the American Future Combat System (FCS), which may appear to the reader to be the most revolutionary armored vehicle system being developed. While the FCS does posit an enhancement over existing vehicles, that enhancement is primarily in the field of digitization, which is covered later. In other areas of tank performance, such as armor protection and firepower, there has not been so rapid a gain.

38. The development of tanks earlier in World War I and during the post-World War I period was even more rapid. See van Creveld, *The Changing Face of War*, pp. 74-75.

39. *Russian Warrior.com*, "History, Development, and Use of the T-54/55 Medium Tank," available from *www.russianwarrior. com/STMMain.htm?1947vehicle_t55history.htm&1*.

40. FAS Military Analysis Network, "T62 Series Tanks," updated September 19, 1999, available from *www.fas.org/man/ dod-101/sys/land/row/t62tank.htm*; *Russian Warrior.com*, "T-62 Main Battle Tank," available from *www.russianwarrior.com/STMMain. htm?1969vehicle_t62main.htm&1*.

41. Gary Cooke, "T-64 Main Battle Tank," 2008, available from *www.inetres.com/gp/military/cv/tank/T-64.html*; *Global Security. org*, "T-64 Tank," available from *www.globalsecurity.org/military/ world/russia/t-64.htm*; Kharkiv Morozov Machine Building Design Bureau, "T-64," available from *morozov.com.ua/eng/body/tanks/t-64*.

php; Kharkiv Morozov Machine Building Design Bureau, "T-64B Main Battle Tank," available from *www.morozov.com.ua/eng/body/tanks/t-64b.php*; The Military Factory, "T-64-Military Tanks, Vehicles and Artillery," available from *www.militaryfactory.com/armor/detail.asp?armor_id=213*; *Warfare.Ru*, "T-64 MBT," available from *Warfare.Ru/?lang=&catid=244&linkid=1774*.

42. This seems to almost mirror the development of the F-16 as a low cost alternative to the F-15.

43. Gary Cooke, "T-72 Main Battle Tank," updated August 18, 2006, available from *www.inetres.com/gp/military/cv/tank/T-72.html*; *Global Security.org*, "T-72 Medium Tank," available from *www.globalsecurity.org/military/world/russia/t-72.htm*.

44. *Global Security.org*, "T-80 Tank," available from *www.globalsecurity.org/military/world/russia/t-80.htm*.

45. *Global Security.org*, "T-90," available from *www.globalsecurity.org/military/world/russia/t-90.htm*.

46. *Russian Warrior.com*, "History, Development, and Use of the T-54/55 Medium Tank."

47. *Ibid.*

48. FAS Military Analysis Network, "T62 Series Tanks"; *Russian Warrior.com*, "T-62 Main Battle Tank."

49. Cooke, "T-64 Main Battle Tank"; *Global Security.org*, "T-64 Tank"; Kharkiv Morozov Machine Building Design Bureau, "T-64"; Kharkiv Morozov Machine Building Design Bureau, "T-64B Main Battle Tank"; The Military Factory, "T-64-Military Tanks, Vehicles and Artillery"; *Warfare.Ru*, "T-64 MBT."

50. Cooke, "T-72 Main Battle Tank"; *Global Security.org*, "T-72 Medium Tank."

51. *Global Security.org*, "T-80 Tank"; *Warfare.Ru*, "T-80UM1 Bars MBT," available from *Warfare.Ru/?catid=244&linkid=1779*.

52. *Global Security.org*, "T-90."

53. The likely reason for this being that during this period the concept of a single main battle tank had not yet been accepted, and development in heavy tanks (T-10 series) continued.

54. FAS Military Analysis Network, "T62 Series Tanks"; *Russian Warrior.com*, "History, Development, and Use of the T-54/55 Medium Tank"; *Russian Warrior.com*, "T-62 Main Battle Tank."

55. Cooke, "T-64 Main Battle Tank"; Cooke, "T-72 Main Battle Tank"; *Global Security.org*, "T-64 Tank"; *Global Security.org*, "T-72 Medium Tank"; *Global Security.org*, "T-80 Tank"; *Global Security.org*, "T-90"; Kharkiv Morozov Machine Building Design Bureau, "T-64"; Kharkiv Morozov Machine Building Design Bureau, "T-64B Main Battle Tank"; The Military Factory, "T-64-Military Tanks, Vehicles and Artillery"; *Warfare.Ru*, "T-64 MBT"; *Warfare.Ru*, "T-80UM1 Bars MBT."

56. Robb McLeod, "Modern Explosive Reactive Armors," 1998, available from *russianarmor.info/Tanks/EQP/era.html*.

57. Kharkiv Morozov Machine Building Design Bureau, "T-64B Main Battle Tank"; Andreas Parsch, "Ford M13/MGM-51 Shillelagh," 2002, available from *www.designation-systems.net/dusrm/m-51.html*.

58. Vladimir Ivanova, "Active Protection for Tanks," 1997, available from *milparade.udm.ru/23/040.htm*; *Warfare.Ru*, "DROZD ACTIVE PROTECTION SYSTEMS," available from *Warfare.Ru/?linkid=2437&catid=314*.

59. Cooke, "T-72 Main Battle Tank"; Defense Update, "Add-on-Reactive Armor Suites," 2004, available from *www.defense-update.com/features/du-1-04/reactive-armor.htm*; Defense Update, "ARENA-E Active Protection System for AFV," updated July 26, 2006, available from *www.defense-update.com/products/a/arena-e.htm*; Ivanova, "Active Protection for Tanks"; McLeod, "Modern Explosive Reactive Armors."

60. *Global Security.org*, "T-80 Tank."

61. Kharkiv Morozov Machine Building Design Bureau, "T-64."

62. *Global Security.org*, "T-72 Medium Tank."

63. Patton-Mania, "Index," available from *www.patton-mania. com/index.html.*

64. And it is likely the Abrams will serve until 2050, 70 years after entering service: Robert Williams, "Armor: Strong Today, Strong Tomorrow," *Armor*, Vol. CXVI, No. 2, March-April 2007, p. 20.

65. Charles Lindblom, *The Policy-Making Process*, Englewood Cliffs, NJ: Prentice-Hall, 1968; Charles Lindblom, "Still Muddling, Not Yet Through," *Public Administration Review*, November/ December 1979.

66. Naval Sea Systems Command, "Historical Review of Cruiser Characteristics, Roles and Missions," updated March 28, 2005, available from *www.aandc.org/research/cruisers/cr_navsea. html#LinkTarget_8557.*

67. "Leander Class," available from *www.battleships-cruisers. co.uk/leander_class.htm.*

68. "Dido Class," available from *www.battleships-cruisers.co.uk/ dido_class.htm.*

69. *Global Security.org*, "CL-55 Cleveland," available from *www.globalsecurity.org/military/systems/ship/cl-55.htm.*

70. *Global Security.org*, "CA-134 Des Moines," available from *www.globalsecurity.org/military/systems/ship/ca-134.htm.*

71. Andrew Toppan, "US Cruisers List: Guided Missile Cruisers," updated July 17, 2000, available from *www.hazegray. org/navhist/cruisers/guided.htm.*

72. FAS Military Analysis Network, "CGN 9 Long Beach," 2008, available from *www.fas.org/man/dod-101/sys/ship/cgn-9.htm.*

73. *Global Security.org*, "CG-47 Ticonderoga," available from *www.globalsecurity.org/military/systems/ship/cg-47.htm*.

74. Exemplified by the DDG-1000's "tumblehome" hull design: Christopher Cavas, "A Nuke-Powered DDG?" *DefenseNews*, March 10, 2008, p. 6.

75. See van Creveld, *The Changing Face of War*, pp. 74-190.

76. Gayle Putrich, "VH-71 Presidential Helicopter On Hold," *DefenseNews*, December 17, 2007, p. 3. Andrew Chuter, "BAE Nears Completion Of New U.K. Nuclear Sub," *DefenseNews*, May 14, 2007, p. 3; Pierre Tran, "EADS Chief Outlines Plans to Ease Dollar Woes," *DefenseNews*, January 14, 2008, p. 9. These are just some of the more recent examples in the public sphere.

77. John Keegan, *A History of Warfare*, London: Huchinson, 1993), p. 344. This tactical-technological stasis occurred, however, in the context of major strategic changes, notably the French Revolution.

78. MacGregor Knox and Williamson Murray, eds., *The Dynamics of Military Revolution 1300-2050,* Cambridge: Cambridge University Press, 2001.

79. John Stone, "The British Army and the Tank," in Theo Farrell and Terry Terriff, eds., *The Sources of Military Change: Culture, Politics, Technology*, Boulder, CO: Lynne Rienner Publishers, 2002, p. 187. See also Keegan, *A History of Warfare*, p. 22.

80. Andrew Gordon, *The Rules of the Game : Jutland and British Naval Command*, Annapolis, MD: Naval Institute Press, 1996; Robert Massie, *Castles of Steel: Britain, Germany, and the Winning of the Great War at Sea*, New York: Random House, 2003; Robert Massie, *Dreadnought: Britain, Germany, and the Coming of the Great War*, New York: Ballantine Books, 1992.

81. Keegan, *A History of Warfare*, p. 225.

82. van Creveld, *The Changing Face of War*, p. 9.

83. *Ibid.*, pp. 10-11.

84. Emily Goldman, "The Spread of Western Military Models to Ottoman Turkey and Meiji Japan," in Theo Farrell and Terry Terriff, eds., *The Sources of Military Change: Culture, Politics, Technology*, Boulder, CO: Lynne Rienner Publishers, 2002, p. 56.

85. Keegan, *A History of Warfare*, p. 349.

86. *Ibid.*, p. 368.

87. Van Creveld in describing the period at the beginning of the 20th century states it was a time when new inventions "were sprouting like mushrooms out of soil." van Creveld, *The Changing Face of War*, p. 38.

88. *Ibid.*, p. 71.

89. The late 1940s/early-mid 1950s were, in the author's view, the time of greatest military technological innovation during the 20th century, bar the two world wars. It was a time when it seemed new fields of science could solve any problem, be it nuclear powered bombers or unflappable tanks. To gain a basic understanding of the period, a good starting point would be *Popular Science* magazines of the decade concerned.

90. It is difficult to obtain precise figures of the F-15s' CPU, but it is known that the system was similar to the AP101 on the Shuttle, as well as the IBM System 360. See Roscoe Ferguson and William Smithgall, "Evolution of the Space Shuttle AP101," 2006, available from *www.klabs.org/mapld06/abstracts/140_ferguson_a. html*; *Global Security.org*, "F-15 Eagle Service Life"; Guy Macon, "Discussion on 8051 performance," available from *www.groupsrv. com/computers/about54200.html*.

91. Data on the F-22's processor speed could not be obtained. *F22Fighter.com*, "F22 Avionics," available from *www.f22fighter. com/avionics.htm#2.1%20Common%20Integrated%20Processor%20* (CIP); *Global Security.org*, "F-22 Raptor Avionics," available from *www.globalsecurity.org/military/systems/aircraft/f-22-avionics.htm*.

92. *Military Aerospace and Avionics*, "F-35 Jet Fighters to Take Integrated Avionics to a Whole New Level," updated May 2003, available from *mae.pennnet.com/articles/article_display.cfm?article_id=175510*.

93. D. G. Kiely, *Defense Procurement: The Equipment Buying Process*, London: Tri-Service Press, 1990, pp. 108-09.

94. These were the specifications of the author's first personal computer (PC), purchased in 1991.

95. Theo Farrell and Terry Terriff, "The Sources of Military Change," in Theo Farrell and Terry Terriff, eds., *The Sources of Military Change: Culture, Politics, Technology*, Boulder, CO: Lynne Rienner Publishers, 2002. Also see van Creveld, *The Changing Face of War*.

96. U.S. Centennial of Flight Commission, "Jet Engines," available from *www.centennialofflight.gov/essay/Evolution_of_Technology/jet_engines/Tech24.htm*.

97. *Flight Journal*, "Engine supercharging," 1998, available from *findarticles.com/p/articles/mi_qa3897/is_199812/ai_n8815045*.

98. *Beyond Discovery*, "GPS: The Role of Atomic Clocks," available from *www.beyonddiscovery.org/content/view.article.asp?a=458*; *GIS Development*, "History of GPS," available from *www.gisdevelopment.net/history/links/gps.htm*; *GPS World*, "GPS Development Timeline," available from *www.gpsworld.com/gpsworld/GPS-Development-Timeline/static/detail/7956*.

99. Doug Richardson, "The Cots Revolution," *Armada*, October 1, 2002, available from *www.accessmylibrary.com/coms2/summary_0286-26978898_ITM*.

100. Farrell and Terriff, "The Sources of Military Change," pp. 7-16. Terry Pierce, *Warfighting and Disruptive Technologies: Disguising Innovation*, London: Frank Cass, 2004, pp. 9-12.

101. Elizabeth Kier, *Imagining War: French and British Military Doctrine Between the Wars*, Princeton, NJ: Princeton University

Press, 1997; Pierce, *Warfighting and Disruptive Technologies*; Barry Posen, *The Sources of Military Doctrine: France, Britain and Germany Between the World Wars*, New York, NY: Cornell University Press, 1984; Stephen Rosen, *Winning the Next War: Innovation and the Modern Military*, Ithaca: Cornell University Press, 1991.

102. There are two main assumptions here, both of which could be questioned: first, that militaries are state-controlled entities; and second, that a state/government has an inherent desire to avoid destruction.

103. Charles Darwin, *On the Origin of Species by Means of Natural Selection*, Peterborough: Broadview Press, 2003.

104. van Creveld, *The Changing Face of War*, p. 149.

105. Kier, *Imagining War*, pp. 26,144.

106. Jeremy Black, "Military Change in Historical Perspective," in Theo Farrell and Terry Terriff, eds., *The Sources of Military Change: Culture, Politics, Technology*, Boulder, CO: Lynne Rienner Publishers, 2002; Farrell and Terriff, "The Sources of Military Change"; Goldman, "The Spread of Western Military Models to Ottoman Turkey and Meiji Japan."

107. William Owens, "Creating a U.S. Military Revolution," in Theo Farrell and Terry Terriff, eds., *The Sources of Military Change: Culture, Politics, Technology*, Boulder, CO: Lynne Rienner Publishers, 2002, p. 205. This is not to say that they are entirely rational, as will become clearer later, but that by and large responses are oriented at an external threat, albeit heavily modified by internal cultural factors such as service pride. See Davis Bobrow, "Components of Defense Policy," in Davis Bobrow, ed., *Components of Defense Policy*, Chicago, IL: Rand McNally & Co, 1965; William Cohen, "The US Senate and the Presidency," in Robert Pfaltzgraff, Jr., and Uri Ra'anan, eds., *National Security Policy: The Decision-Making Process*, Hamden, CT: Archon Books, 1984; Constantine Danopolous and Daniel Zirker, eds., *Civil-Military Relations in the Soviet and Yugoslav Successor States*, Boulder, CO: Westview Press, 1996; Lewis Dexter, "Congressmen and the Making of Military Policy," in Davis Bobrow, ed., *Components of Defense Policy*, Chicago, IL: Rand McNally & Co, 1965; John Endicott, "The

National Security Council: Formalised Coordination and Policy Planning," in Pfaltzgraff and Ra'anan, eds., *National Security Policy*; Gregory Flynn, ed., *Soviet Military Doctrine and Western Policy*, London: Routledge, 1989; J. Ronald Fox and James Field, *The Defense Management Challenge: Weapons Acquisition*, Boston, MA: Harvard University Press, 1988; Christopher Gibson and Don Snider, "Civil-Military Relations and the Potential to Influence: A Look at the National Security Decision-Making Process," *Armed Forces and Society*, Vol. 25, No. 2, Winter 1999; William Green and Theodore Karasik, eds., *Gorbachev and His Generals : The Reform of Soviet Military Doctrine*, Boulder, CO: Westview Press, 1990; Michael Hobkirk, "Policy Planning and Resource Allocation in the U.S. Deparment of Defense: An Outsider's View," in Pfaltzgraff and Ra'anan, eds., *National Security Policy*; Samuel P. Huntington, "Strategic Planning and the Political Process," in Davis Bobrow, ed., *Components of Defense Policy*, Chicago, IL: Rand McNally & Co, 1965; S. Robert Lichter and Stanley Rothman, "The Media and National Defense," in Pfaltzgraff and Ra'anan, eds., *National Security Policy*; Gene Lyons, "The New Civil-Military Relations," in Davis Bobrow, ed., *Components of Defense Policy*, Chicago, IL: Rand McNally & Co, 1965; William Odom, *The Collapse of the Soviet Military*, New Haven, CT: Yale University Press, 1998; P. A. Phalon, "Government-Industry Relations and Defense Decision Making," in Pfaltzgraff and Ra'anan, eds., *National Security Policy*; Pierce, *Warfighting and Disruptive Technologies: Disguising Innovation*; Posen, *The Sources of Military Doctrine: France, Britain and Germany Between the World Wars*; Roger Reese, *The Soviet Military Experience : A History of the Soviet Army, 1917-1991*, London: Routledge, 2001; Stephen Rosen, *War and Human Nature*, Princeton, NJ: Princeton University Press, 2005; Warner Schilling, "The Politics of National Defense: Fiscal 1950," in Warner Schilling, Paul Hammond, and Glenn Snyder, eds., *Strategy, Politics and Defense Budgets*, New York, NY: Columbia University Press, 1966; Glenn Snyder, "The 'New Look' of 1953," in Schilling, Hammond, and Snyder, eds., *Strategy, Politics and Defense Budget*; Nikolai Sokov, *Russian Strategic Modernization: The Past and Future*, Lanham: Rowman & Littlefield 1999; Franklin Spinney, *Defense Facts of Life: The Plan/ Reality Mismatch*, Boulder, CO: Westview Press, 1985; Richard White, "Congressional Limitations and Oversight of Executive Decision-making Power: The Influence of the Members and the Staff," in Pfaltzgraff and Ra'anan, eds., *National Security Policy*.

108. Aviation Explorer, "NASA/USAF XB-70 VALKYRIE-Strategic Experimental Bomber Aircraft History, Pictures and Facts," available from *www.aviationexplorer.com/xb-70_facts.htm*; Boeing, "XB-70A Valkyrie Research Aircraft," available from *www.boeing.com/history/bna/xb70.htm*.

109. Airforce Technology, "MiG-25P Foxbat Interceptor Aircraft, Russia," available from *www.airforce-technology.com/projects/mig25/*; *Global Security.org*, "MiG-25 Foxbat." Recent assertions by Russian scientists indicate that the American A-12 rather than the XB-70 was the perceived target of the MiG-25, but that is irrelevant to the argument at hand, as it was still a deliberate technological counter.

110. *Global Security.org*, "Moskit SS-N-22 Sunburn."

111. It might be said the trends of the Cold War are merely continuations of post-1945 trends: van Creveld, *The Changing Face of War*, pp. 197-98.

112. J. Simpson, "Achieving Nuclear Weapons Non-Proliferation and Non-Possession: Problems and Prospects," in Robert Patman, ed., Security in a Post-Cold War World, Basingstoke: Macmillan, 1999, pp. 145-147.

113. Richard Lacquement, Jr., *Shaping American Capabilities After the Cold War*, Westport, CT: Praeger, 2003, pp. 60-94; Anne Aldis and Roger McDermott, eds., *Russian Military Reform 1992-2002*, London: Frank Cass, 2003.

114. Benjamin Miller, "Hot War, Cold Peace: An International-Regional Synthesis," in Zeev Maoz and Azar Gat, eds., *War in a Changing World*, Michigan: University of Michigan Press, 2001, pp. 104-122, has an interesting analysis of the causes and courses of such conflicts.

115. Francis Fukuyama, "The End of History," *The National Interest,* Summer 1989.

116. See Chapter Two of Zhivan Alach, "Peace Support Operations: International Evolution and New Zealand

Adaptation," MA, University of Auckland, 2002. Also see Chapter Two of Zhivan Alach, "Facing New Challenges: Adapting the NZDF and ADF to the Post-Cold War Security Environment," University of Auckland, 2006.

117. Aldis and McDermott, eds., *Russian Military Reform 1992-2002*; Jennifer Mathers, "Reform and the Russian Military," in Theo Farrell and Terry Terriff, eds., *The Sources of Military Change: Culture, Politics, Technology*, Boulder, CO: Lynne Rienner Publishers, 2002; Sokov, *Russian Strategic Modernization: The Past and Future*. These sources provide good starting points for a closer examination of the issues faced by Russian/Soviet military technology in the post-Cold War period.

118. Mathers, "Reform and the Russian Military."

119. ROSOBORONEKSPORT, "Index," available from *www.roe.ru/*.

120. An excellent way of seeing how these trends have developed is to survey the following: International Institute for Strategic Studies, *The Military Balance*, Abingdon: Taylor & Francis for the IISS, 1992-2007.

121. This can be seen through a cursory skim of recent issues of such periodicals as *DefenseNews*.

122. Lacquement, *Shaping American Capabilities After the Cold War*, pp. 60-78.

123. Carl Conetta and Charles Knight, "Post-Cold War US Military Expenditure in the Context of World Spending Trends," 1997, available from *www.comw.org/pda/bmemo10.htm*; Steven Kosiak and Elizabeth Heeter, "Post-Cold War Defense Spending Cuts: A Bipartisan Decision," 2000, available from *www.csbaonline.org/4Publications/PubLibrary/H.20000831.Post-Cold_War_Defe/H.20000831.Post-Cold_War_Defe.php*; Stephen Shalom, "The V-22 OSPREY and the post-Cold War Military Budget," updated June 1993, available from *www.zmag.org/zmag/articles/shalomosprey.html*.

124. Lacquement, *Shaping American Capabilities After the Cold War*, pp. 20-25.

125. By elongation is meant a lengthening of development timeframes and a reduction in production numbers in a specific period of time.

126. *Global Security.org*, "B-2 Production," available from *www.globalsecurity.org/wmd/systems/b-2-production.htm*.

127. Army Technology, "RAH-66 Comanche Reconnaissance/ Attack Helicopter, USA"; *Global Security.org*, "Crusader," available from *www.globalsecurity.org/military/systems/ground/ crusader.htm*; *Global Security.org*, "RAH-66 Comanche"; Vernon Loeb, "Rumsfeld Untracks 'Crusader'," 2002, available from *www. washingtonpost.com/ac2/wp-dyn?pagename=article&node=&contentI d=A53762-2002May8&notFound=true*.

128. Gayle Putrich, "House Panel Slashes FCS, JSF," 2007, available from *www.armytimes.com/news/2007/05/defense_markup_ 070502/*.

129. William Matthews, "U.S. Military Funding Rises Above Party Confrontation," *DefenseNews*, December 17, 2007, pp. 13-14.

130. Andrew Chuter, "Brown: Trim, Delay, Don't Kill Programs," *DefenseNews*, January 14, 2008, pp. 1, 8.

131. Kris Osborn, "New Mind-Set for U.S.Army: Start Tests Sooner," *DefenseNews*, March 10, 2008, p. 4.

132. At first glance this appears counterintuitive, as most would posit that the Reagan-era expansion of military budgets caused technological advancement. Three reasons for its failure to do so can be posited: first, it was too short a period to substantially alter major fields; second, it focused on extremely novel fields of technology where a great deal of raw research was required before progress could be made in the field of applied technology and military applications; and third, much of the funding was focused on quantity and increasing the number of existing platforms rather than necessarily developing new platforms.

133. Useful reading here includes David Bobrow, "Military Security Policy," in R. Kent Weaver and Bert Rockman, eds., *Do Institutions Matter? Government Capabilities in the United States and Abroad*, Washington DC: The Brookings Institution, 1993; Bobrow, "Components of Defense Policy"; Dexter, "Congressmen and the Making of Military Policy"; Endicott, "The National Security Council"; Fox and Field, *The Defense Management Challenge*; Gibson and Snider, "Civil-Military Relations and the Potential to Influence"; Stanley Heginbotham, "Congress and Defense Policy Making: Towards Realistic Expectations in a System of Countervailing Parochialisms," in Pfaltzgraff and Ra'anan, eds., *National Security Policy*; Hobkirk, "Policy Planning and Resource Allocation in the U.S. Deparment of Defense"; Huntington, "Strategic Planning and the Political Process"; Lyons, "The New Civil-Military Relations"; Phalon, "Government-Industry Relations and Defense Decision Making"; Schilling, "The Politics of National Defense"; Spinney, *Defense Facts of Life: The Plan/Reality Mismatch*.

134. This is a general trend only, and there are exceptions. For example, Roman imperial government was larger than governments of the Middle Ages.

135. In that it was carried out in an environment lacking telephones, personal computers, and emails. Much of the communication was by post or in person.

136. See Kiely, *Defense Procurement*, pp. 2-14. This has some discussion on this point. He suggests that such state-controlled systems are actually a liability in the modern period.

137. Encyclopedia Britannica Online, "Planning, Programming, and Budgeting System, or PPBS, economics," available from *www.britannica.com/eb/topic-463163/Planning-Programming-and-Budgeting-System*; Wayne Parsons, *An Introduction to the Theory and Practice of Policy Analysis*, Aldershot: Edward Elgar, 1995, p. 408; U.S. Department of Defense, "DoD's Planning, Programming and Budgeting System," available from *www.mors.org/meetings/cbp/presentations/Gordon_PPBS-Mon.pdf*.

138. It is not merely the United States system that has been criticized for being overly bureaucratic. See Neil James, "The

Bureaucracy's Control over the Australian Defense Force," *National Observer*, Autumn 2001; Neil James, "Whole-of-government reform: A Practical First Step," *Defender*, Vol. XXII, No. 1, Autumn 2005.

139. It might be termed a hexagon if military industry were also included.

140. Hobkirk, "Policy Planning and Resource Allocation in the U.S. Deparment of Defense."

141. Fox and Field, *The Defense Management Challenge*, pp. 80-89.

142. *Ibid.*, pp. 114-115.

143. *Ibid.*, p. 131.

144. See also Lacquement, *Shaping American Capabilities After the Cold War*, pp. 79-136.

145. Spinney, *Defense Facts of Life*, p. 178.

146. *Ibid.*, p. 146.

147. *Ibid.*, p. 108.

148. Gibson and Snider, "Civil-Military Relations and the Potential to Influence: A Look at the National Security Decision-Making Process," p. 193.

149. Huntington, "Strategic Planning and the Political Process."

150. *Ibid.* Also see Bobrow, "Military Security Policy"; Gibson and Snider, "Civil-Military Relations and the Potential to Influence"; Lacquement, *Shaping American Capabilities After the Cold War*. They were also applicable to an earlier period. See Schilling, "The Politics of National Defense." A newer source is Paul Bolt, Damon Coletta, and Collins Shackelford, eds., *American Defense Policy*, Baltimore, MD: John Hopkins University Press, 2005.

151. Huntington, "Strategic Planning and the Political Process," pp. 84-86.

152. Danopolous and Zirker, eds., *Civil-military Relations in the Soviet and Yugoslav Successor States*; Flynn, ed., *Soviet Military Doctrine and Western Policy*; Green and Karasik, eds., *Gorbachev and His Generals*; Odom, *The Collapse of the Soviet Military*; Reese, *The Soviet Military Experience*; Sokov, *Russian Strategic Modernization*. These sources all provide a broad picture of the relevant issues.

153. Mathers, "Reform and the Russian Military," pp. 171-79.

154. Kiely, *Defense Procurement*, p. 14.

155. *Ibid.*, p. 22.

156. Pierre Tran, "Britain, France Wrestle With Outsourcing, Procurement Woes," *DefenseNews*, March 10, 2008, p. 7; Tran, "EADS Chief Outlines Plans to Ease Dollar Woes," p. 9, provide recent examples of this.

157. U.S. Centennial of Flight Commission, "North American Aviation," available from *www.centennialofflight.gov/essay/ Aerospace/NorthAmerican/Aero37.htm*.

158. Northrop Grumman, "Our Heritage," available from *www.northropgrumman.com/heritage/index.html*.

159. Boeing, "The Boeing Company . . . The Giants Merge," available from *www.boeing.com/history/narrative/n079boe.html*.

160. Fairchild is the anomaly, being part of M7 Aerospace. M7 Aerospace, "About M7," available from *www.m7aerospace.com/ page/about.jsp*.

161. Lockheed Martin, "History," available from *www. lockheedmartin.com/aboutus/history/index.html*.

162. William Anders and Nancy Perry, "General Dynamics" Selling Strategy," 1993, available from *money.cnn.com/magazines/ fortune/fortune_archive/1993/01/11/77366/index.htm*.

163. Boeing, "The Boeing Company . . . The Giants Merge."

164. Lockheed Martin, "History."

165. FAS Military Analysis Network, "F-5 Tiger," updated December 27, 1999, available from *www.fas.org/man/dod-101/sys/ac/f-5.htm*.

166. *Global Security.org*, "F-4 Phantom II."

167. Calculations of military inflation often attempt to factor for quality increases, but even then inflation continues to rise unabated: Benjamin Fordham, "The Political and Economic Sources of Inflation in the American Military Budget," *The Journal of Conflict Resolution*, Vol. 47, No. 5, October 2003, p. 578.

168. Pierre Tran, "Paris Vows to Protect Defense Research Budget," *DefenseNews*, January 14, 2008, p. 6.

169. Obaid Younossi, *Is Weapon System Cost Growth Increasing?: A Quantitative Assessment of Completed and Ongoing Programs*, Santa Monica: RAND Corporation, 2007.

170. Fordham, "The Political and Economic Sources of Inflation in the American Military Budget," p. 574; van Creveld, *The Changing Face of War*, p. 202.

171. This 80:20 rule is a modification of the Pareto Principle. F. John Reh, "Pareto's Principle-The 80-20 Rule," available from *management.about.com/cs/generalmanagement/a/Pareto081202.htm*.

172. Fordham, "The Political and Economic Sources of Inflation in the American Military Budget," p. 580.

173. *Ibid.*, p. 585.

174. *Ibid.*, p. 586.

175. Recent examples being Cavas, "A Nuke-Powered DDG?" p. 6; Chuter, "BAE Nears Completion Of New U.K. Nuclear Sub," p. 3; Gregor Ferguson, "Australia Cancels Helicopter Program,"

DefenseNews, March 10, 2008, p. 5; Barbara Opall-Rome, "Israel May Rethink LCS Plans as Costs Soar," *DefenseNews*, January 7, 2008, p. 1.

176. Lacquement, *Shaping American Capabilities After the Cold War*, pp. 48-166. Nor is it only the United States that does so. See Chuter, "Brown: Trim, Delay, Don't Kill Programs," pp. 1, 8.

177. Related issues are discussed in Bennett, "Interview with James Finley," p. 30.

178. Fordham, "The Political and Economic Sources of Inflation in the American Military Budget," pp. 576, 592.

179. Luijkx, "Lockheed F-104 Starfighter Site."

180. Jeremy Black, *War in the New Century*, London: Continuum, 2001, p. 9.

181. Hugh Smith, "The Last Casualty? Public Perceptions of Bearable Cost in a Democracy," in Michael Evans and Alan Ryan, eds., *The Human Face of Warfare*, St Leonards: Allen & Unwin, 2000, pp. 57-83.

182. Some have suggested modern systems no longer fit the traditional mass production industrial paradigm. See van Creveld, *The Changing Face of War*, p. 267.

183. Mathers, "Reform and the Russian Military."

184. Recent examples of complexity causing delays can be seen in Ferguson, "Australia Cancels Helicopter Program," p. 5; Putrich, "VH-71 Presidential Helicopter On Hold," p. 3; Tran, "EADS Chief Outlines Plans to Ease Dollar Woes," p. 9.

185. The following provides an interesting analysis of the issue of complexity, though her focus is different from mine. See Chris Demchak, "Complexity and Theory of Networked Militaries," in Theo Farrell and Terry Terriff, eds., *The Sources of Military Change: Culture, Politics, Technology*, Boulder, CO: Lynne Rienner Publishers, 2002.

186. Rosen, *War and Human Nature*. This discusses many of the human issues that affect defense policymaking, including cognitive limitations.

187. *Global Security.org*, "Stryker Armored Vehicle," available from *www.globalsecurity.org/military/systems/ground/iav.htm*.

188. Defense Update, "Add-on-Reactive Armor Suites"; Defense Update, "Lightweight Armor Protection for Combat Vehicles," 2004, available from *www.defense-update.com/features/du-3-04/feature-light-armor.htm*.

189. Exemplified by the NZ Police's INCIS project: Francis Small, "Ministerial Enquiry into INCIS," updated November 2000, available from *www.courts.govt.nz/pubs/reports/2000/incis_rpt/index.html*.

190. An extension of this argument might be that a major change in the strategic environment, as occurred with the end of the Cold War, would lead to technological slowdown as there would be a substantial pause before the parameters of the new environment could be defined and the requirements to operate in that new environment identified.

191. John Bennett, "Amid Criticism, JIEDDO Stands By Selection Process," *DefenseNews*, January 8, 2008, p. 5; Gina Cavallaro, "U.S. Army Multiplies MRAP Purchase Plans," *DefenseNews*, May 14, 2007, p. 6.

192. "Random Notes," *DefenseNews*, January 14, 2008, p. 18; *Space Daily*, "UAV Development Will Drive Advanced Aerospace Technologies," updated May 30, 2006, available from *www.spacedaily.com/reports/UAV_Development_Will_Drive_Advanced_Aerospace_Technologies.html*; UAV Marketplace, "History of UAVs," available from *www.uavm.com/uavindustry/historicalbackground.html*; Jack Weible, "Casting a Larger Shadow: U.S. Marines Join Army in Training on Popular UAV," *DefenseNews*, January 7, 2008, p. 16.

193. For the programs of two major nations, see United Kingdom Ministry of Defense, "Equipment and Logistics,"

2008, available from *www.mod.uk/DefenseInternet/DefenseNews/ EquipmentAndLogistics/*; U.S. Department of Defense, "DefenseLink," available from *www.defenselink.mil/*.

194. Alexander, *Winning the War*; Bitzinger, *Defense Transformation and the Asia Pacific*; R. Franck, Jr., "Lifting the Fog of War," *Armed Forces and Society*, Vol. 28, No. 1, Fall 2001; Lawrence Freedman, "The Changing Forms of Military Conflict," *Survival*, Vol. 40, No. 4, Winter 1998-99; Dennis Gormley, "Implementing a Revolution in Military Affairs: The United States Quest for Military Reform," in Istvan Gyarmati and Theodor Winkler, eds., *Post-Cold War Defense Reform: Lessons Learned in Europe and the United States*, Washington DC: Brasseys, 2002; National Defense Panel, *Transforming Defense: National Security in the 21st Century*, 1997, available from *www.fas.org/man/docs/ndp/part04.htm*; Owens, "Creating a U.S. Military Revolution"; Andrew Ross *et al.*, "What Do We Mean By 'Transformation'?" *Naval War College Review*, Vol. 55, No. 1, Winter 2002; Elinor Sloan, *The Revolution in Military Affairs: Implications for Canada and NATO*, Montreal: McGill-Queens University, 2002. The above provide a good range of views on the issues of the RMA.

195. John English, "Balancing Deep and Close Battle: Will We Still Close with the Enemy?" in Michael Evans and Alan Ryan, eds., *The Human Face of Warfare*, St Leonards: Allen & Unwin, 2000, pp. 98-99.

196. van Creveld, *The Changing Face of War*, p. 246.

197. Franck,"Lifting the Fog of War"; National Defense Panel, *Transforming Defense*.

198. Bruce Berkowitz, *The New Face Of War*, New York: Free Press, 2003, p. 102.

199. Gray, *Strategy for Chaos*, pp. 55-56; Knox and Murray, eds., *The Dynamics of Military Revolution 1300-2050*.

200. van Creveld, *The Changing Face of War*, p. 204.

201. *Ibid.*, pp. 99-101.

202. While it is not fashionable today to refer specifically to the RMA in such terms, the constant focus on "transformation" — the newer and politically acceptable term — among policymakers and academics suggests that many still support the integral concepts of the RMA.

203. Alexander, *Winning the War*; Lacquement, *Shaping American Capabilities After the Cold War*; Douglas MacGregor, *Transformation Under Fire: Revolutionizing How America Fights*, Westport, CT: Praeger, 2003. These are just three writers who suggest that the United States has definitely not transformed. In the period since they wrote that the United States has been increasingly focused on operational requirements in Iraq and Afghanistan rather than long-term transformation issues.

204. It might be posited that an RMA force could also have a high manpower-to-area ratio but such would seem to be inherently contradictory. The RMA is about small, powerful forces, not mass infantry. Also, even if such a force were possible, it is unclear how the RMA-aspects of it — precision sensor-shooter networks, for example — would be of great advantage in counterinsurgency or peace support operations.

205. Berkowitz, *The New Face Of War*, p. 98; J. Gentry, "Doomed to Fail: America's Blind Faith in Military Technology," *Parameters*, Vol. 32, No. 4, Winter 2002/03; MacGregor, *Transformation Under Fire*, pp. 52-56.

206. The rate of advance of American forces, however, was no swifter than that of Army Group Centre in 1941. See van Creveld, *The Changing Face of War*, pp. 130-31.

207. Jayson Altieri, "Counterinsurgency Operations in Iraq," *Armor*, Vol. 115, No. 3, May-June 2006; Nigel Aylwin-Foster, "Changing the Army for Counterinsurgency Operations," *Military Review*, Vol. 86, No. 6, November-December 2005; Kevin Benson, "OIF Phase IV: A Planner's Reply to Brigadier Aylwin-Foster," *Military Review*, March-April 2006; Walter J. Boyne, *Operation IRAQI FREEDOM: What Went Right, What Went Wrong, And Why*, New York: Forge, 2003; Daniel Byman and Kenneth Pollack, *Things Fall Apart: What do we do if Iraq implodes*, Brookings

Institution, 2006; Peter Chiarelli, Patrick Michaelis, and Geoffrey Norman, "Armor in Urban Terrain: The Critical Enabler," *Armor*, March-April 2005; Anthony Cordesman, *Iraqi Security Forces: A Strategy for Success*, Westport, CT: Praeger Security International, 2006; Michael Eisenstadt and Jeffrey White, "Assessing Iraq's Sunni Arab Insurgency," *Military Review*, Vol. 86, No. 3, May-June 2006; Mark Etherington, *Revolt on the Tigris*, London: Hurst & Company, 2005; James Greer, "Operation Knockout: Counterinsurgency in Iraq," *Military Review*, Vol. 85, No. 6, November-December 2005; Carl Grunow, "Advising Iraqis: Building the Iraqi Army," *Military Review*, July-August 2006; Matt Hilburn, "Policing the Insurgents," *Sea Power*, Vol. 49, No. 3, March 2006; "Iraq Update," *Army*, Vol. 55, No. 12, December 2005; Frederick Kagan, "Iraq Is Not Vietnam," *Policy Review*, Vol. 134, December-January 2005/06; Michael Knights, *Cradle of Conflict: Iraq and the Birth of the Modern U.S. Military*, Annapolis, MD: Naval Institute Press, 2005; Timothy Lomperis, "To a Baghdad Victory via Saigon," *World Affairs*, Vol. 168, No. 4, Spring 2006; Morgan Mann, "Steps to Winning," *Marine Corps Gazette*, Vol. 90, No. 3, March 2006; Douglas Ollivant and Eric Chewning, "Producing Victory: Rethinking Conventional Forces in COIN Operations," *Military Review*, July-August 2006; Norman Solomon, "The Bogus Blurring of Terrorism and Insurgency in Iraq," *The Humanist*, Vol. 66, No. 2, March-April 2006; Staff of the Marine Corps Center for Lessons Learned, "Operation Iraqi Freedom Lessons Learned," *Marine Corps Gazette*, Vol. 89, No. 5, May 2005; Gregory Starace, "Status of the Iraqi Security Force," *Marine Corps Gazette*, Vol. 89, No. 12, December 2005; Francis "Bing" West, "American Military Performance in Iraq," *Military Review*, September-October 2006; David Zucchino, *Thunder Run: The Armored Strike to Capture Baghdad*, New York: Atlantic Monthly Press, 2004.

208. Gray, *Strategy for Chaos*, p. 8.

209. Black, *War in the New Century*, p. 111.

210. Gentry, "Doomed to Fail."

211. The reader is invited to look at Evans, "Clausewitz's Chameleon," p. 33.

212. Colin Gray, "How Has War Changed Since the End of the Cold War?" *Parameters*, Spring 2005; Lonsdale, *The Nature of War in the Information Age.*

213. Richard Shultz and Andreas Vogt, "The Real Intelligence Failure on 9/11 and the Case for a Doctrine of Striking First," in Russell Howard and Reid Sawyer, eds., *Terrorism and Counterterrorism: Understanding the New Security Environment*, Guilford, CT: McGraw-Hill/Dushkin, 2004, pp. 408-420.

214. Evans, "Clausewitz's Chameleon"; Douglas MacGregor, "Resurrecting Transformation for the Post-Industrial Era," in Evans *et al.*, eds., *Future Armies, Future Challengers*; Ryan, "Land Forces in 21st Century Coalition Operations"; Roger Spiller, "Sharp Corners: Combat Operations in Urban Areas," in Evans *et al.*, eds., *Future Armies, Future Challengers.*

215. Since the end of the Cold War, the chance of a French soldier seeing action, for example, has increased at least eight-fold. Bernard Boene and Michel Martin, "France: In the Throes of Epoch-Making Change," in Charles Moskos, John Williams, and David Segal, eds., *The Postmodern Military: Armed Forces after the Cold War*, New York: Oxford University Press, 2000, pp. 60-61.

216. One only needs to read the major defense policy documents of the United States, United Kingdom, and Australia in the period since 1991 to see how strongly that perception was held.

217. Deborah Avant and James Lebovic, "U.S. Military Responses to Post-Cold War Missions," in Theo Farrell and Terry Terriff, eds., *The Sources of Military Change: Culture, Politics, Technology*, Boulder, CO: Lynne Rienner Publishers, 2002, pp. 143-57. This notes the attitudes of U.S. military personnel in this regard. See also van Creveld, *The Changing Face of War*, p. 196.

218. Keegan, *A History of Warfare*, is the essential source here, but also see Theo Farrell and Terry Terriff, eds., *The Sources of Military Change: Culture, Politics, Technology*, Boulder, CO: Lynne Rienner Publishers, 2002; Rupert Smith, *The Utility of Force*, London: Allen Lane, 2005.

219. C. E. Callwell, *Small Wars: Their Principles and Practice*, Lincoln: University of Nebraska Press, 1906/1996.

220. Stanford Encyclopedia of Philosophy, "Socrates," 2005, available from *plato.stanford.edu/entries/socrates/*.

221. Peter Hunter Blair, *An Introduction to Anglo-Saxon England*, Cambridge: Cambridge University Press, 2003.

222. Reginald Allen Brown, *The Normans*, Woodbridge: Boydell Press, 1994.

223. J. F. C. Fuller, *The Generalship of Alexander the Great*, London: Eyre & Spottiswoode, 1958.

224. Keegan, *A History of Warfare*, p. 293; "The Sack of Constantinople," *www.roman-empire.net/constant/1203-1204.html*.

225. Keegan, *A History of Warfare*, pp. 210-211.

226. Klaus Gautzel and Torsten Schwinghammer, *Warfare Since the Second World War*, New Brunswick, NJ: Transaction, 2000.

227. A. Adebajo and C. Landsberg, "Back to the Future: United Nations Peacekeeping in Africa," in A. Adebajo and C. L. Sriram, eds., *Managing Armed Conflicts in the 21st Century*, London: Frank Cass, 2001, p. 166; J. Boulden, *Peace Enforcement: The UN Experience in Congo, Somalia, and Bosnia*, Westport, CT: Praeger, 2001, pp. 25-39; J. Matthew-Vaccaro, "United Nations Peace Operations in the Congo: Decolonialism and Superpower Conflict in the Guise of United Nations Peacekeeping," in John T. Fishel, ed., *The Savage Wars of Peace: Towards a New Paradigm of Peace Operations*, Boulder, CO: Westview Press, 1998.

228. P. Shearman, "NATO Expansion and the Russian Question," in Robert Patman, ed., *Security in a Post-Cold War World*, Basingstoke: Macmillan, 1999, pp. 161-171.

229. It might be said that there has been an over-correction from focus on conventional to nonconventional issues.

230. The following sections are partly derived from Alach, "Facing New Challenges: Adapting the NZDF and ADF to the Post-Cold War Security Environment."

231. John Richardson, "Strategic Thinking in an Era of Intervention: Thinking Out of a Box with No Sides," *Comparative Strategy*, No. 181999, pp. 32-46.

232. Freedman, "The Changing Forms of Military Conflict," p. 53; Prakash Mirchandrai, "The Army and the Media," *Australian Army Journal, Land Warfare Studies Centre*, Vol. 1, No. 1, June 2003, pp. 60-65; Munkler, *The New Wars*, p. 90; Smith, "The Last Casualty?" p. 64.

233. Reuben Bowd, *Doves Over The Pacific: In Pursuit of Peace and Stability in Bougainville*, Loftus: Australian Military History Publications, 2007; Bob Breen, *Give Peace a Chance: Operation LAGOON, Bougainville 1994: A Case Study of Military Action and Diplomacy*, Canberra: Strategic and Defense Studies Centre, Australian National University, 2001; Karl Claxton, *Bougainville 1988-1998: Five Searches for Security in the North Solomons Province of Papua New Guinea*, Canberra: ANU Strategic and Defense Studies Centre, 1998; *Bougainville Peace Process*, August 6; J. Rolfe, "Peacekeeping the Pacific Way in Bougainville," *International Peacekeeping*, Vol. 8, No. 4, Winter 2001; Natascha Spark and Jackie Bailey, "Disarmament in Bougainville: Guns in Boxes," *International Peacekeeping*, Vol. 12, No. 4, Winter 2005; D. H. Warmuff, "New Zealand's Role in the Bougainville Crisis: A Case Study in Conflict," *New Zealand Army Journal*, Vol. 21, July 1999.

234. A range of sources useful here include David Carment and Patrick James, "International Ethnopolitics: Theory, Peacekeeping, and Policy," in J. Stack, Jr., and L. Hebron, eds., *The Ethnic Entanglement: Conflict and Intervention in World Politics*, Westport, CT: Praeger, 1999; Sheila Croucher, "Constructing the Ethnic Spectacle: Identity Politics in a Postmodern World," in John Stack, Jr., and Lui Hebron, eds., *The Ethnic Entanglement: Conflict and Intervention in World Politics*, Westport, CT: Praeger, 1999; Ivan Gabal, "Ethnic Strife in Post-Communist Europe," in Nato Defense College, ed., *Co-Operative Security Arrangements in Europe*, Frankfurt am Main: P Lang, 1997; Munkler, *The New Wars*; John

Stack, Jr., and Lui Hebron, "The Internationalization of Ethnicity: The Crisis of Legitimacy and Authority in World Politics," in John Stack, Jr., and Lui Hebron, eds., *The Ethnic Entanglement: Conflict and Intervention in World Politics*, Westport, CT: Praeger, 1999; John Stack, Jr., and Lui Hebron, "World Politics and the Internationalization of Ethnicity: The Challenge of Primordial and Structural Perspectives," in John Stack, Jr., and Lui Hebron, eds., *The Ethnic Entanglement: Conflict and Intervention in World Politics*, Westport, CT: Praeger, 1999.

235. Magnus Ranstorp, "Terrorism in the Name of Religion," in Russell Howard and Reid Sawyer, eds., *Terrorism and Counterterrorism: Understanding the New Security Environment*, Guilford, CT: McGraw-Hill/Dushkin, 2004, pp. 125-132; Martin Shubik, "Terrorism, Technology, and the Socioeconomics of Death," *Comparative Strategy*, Vol. 16, No. 4, October/December 1997. These discuss issues relating to Cold War and post-Cold War terrorism.

236. Adam Dolnik, "All God's Poisons: Reevaluating the Threat of Religious Terrorism with Respect to Nonconventional Weapons," in Russell Howard and Reid Sawyer, eds., *Terrorism and Counterterrorism: Understanding the New Security Environment*, Guilford, CT: McGraw-Hill/Dushkin, 2004, pp. 161-68.

237. Robert Bent, "Military Forces Survivability in a Weapons of Mass Destruction Environment," in William Schilling, ed., Nontraditional Warfare: Twenty-First-Century Threats and Responses, Dulles, VA: Brasseys, 2002; Malcolm Davis and Colin Gray, "Weapons of Mass Destruction," in John Baylis *et al.*, eds., *Strategy in the Contemporary World*, Oxford: Oxford University Press, 2002; Dolnik, "All God's Poisons"; Richard Pilch, "The Bioterrorist Threat in the United States," in Russell Howard and Reid Sawyer, eds., *Terrorism and Counterterrorism: Understanding the New Security Environment*, Guilford, CT: McGraw-Hill/ Dushkin, 2004; William Schilling, "Nontraditional Warfare Threats," in William Schilling, ed., *Nontraditional Warfare: Twenty-First-Century Threats and Responses*, Dulles, VA: Brasseys, 2002; Simpson, "Achieving Nuclear Weapons Non-Proliferation and Non-Possession: Problems and Prospects"; Jessica Stern, "Getting and Using the Weapons," in Russell Howard and Reid Sawyer, eds., *Terrorism and Counterterrorism: Understanding the New Security Environment*, Guilford, CT: 2004.

238. Black, *War in the New Century*, p. 9.

239. It is far from settled, however, and the following provide a good taster of the possibilities: Alexander, *Winning the War: Advanced Weapons, Strategies and Concepts for the Post 9/11 World*; Berkowitz, *The New Face Of War*; Les Brownlee and Peter Schoomaker, "Serving a Nation at War: A Campaign Quality Army with Joint and Expeditionary Capabilities," *Parameters*, Summer 2004; A. Cohen, "Russia, Islam and the War on Terrorism: An Uneasy Future," *Demokratizatsiya*, Vol. 10, No. 4, Fall 2002; Garamone, "Mullen Addresses Rapid Change, Other Issues at Australian War College"; Gray, "How Has War Changed Since the End of the Cold War?"; Lonsdale, *The Nature of War in the Information Age: Clausewitzian Future*; Jasner Lupo, "Development of Smart Sensorwebs for Future Warfare Operations," in William Schilling, ed., *Nontraditional Warfare: Twenty-First-Century Threats and Responses*, Dulles, VA: Brasseys, 2002; Mahnken, "The American Way of War in the Twenty-First Century"; Ollivant and Chewning, "Producing Victory."

240. And as noted earlier, the Abrams tank, developed in the 1970s, may still be in service then also.